MICHAEL CUSACK AND THE GAA is a full-length
biographical story of one of the neglected pioneers of the modern
Irish cultural and political revival.

Born in Carron, in the remote Burren area of north Clare,
Cusack became a teacher, a career which he pursued in all four
provinces before settling in Dublin where he founded his own Academy.
In the ten years from 1877 to 1887, he made his mark on Irish
athletics, revived the national game of hurling which was almost extinct,
took part in a seminal move to restore the Irish language, edited
a new Irish weekly newspaper, and founded the GAA.

He was a colourful character, given to boasting, full of
prejudices of all kinds, with a voice of stentorian dimensions, and his
manner, dress and general deportment made him impossible to ignore.
He was the model for 'the Citizen' in James Joyce's *Ulysses*.

MARCUS de BÚRCA was chosen to write the official history
of the GAA to celebrate the centenary of its founding.
THE GAA: A History first appeared in 1980, with a shorter version in Irish
in 1984. There followed two minor works; one on the Leinster Council,
the other on a famous Dublin club, which won a major centenary
award for books on the GAA. He has also published *John O'Leary*
and *The O'Rahilly*.

A graduate of both UCD and King's Inns, he was a journalist and
practising barrister in the 1950s, then spent over twenty-five years in
the Attorney General's office, as chief parliamentary draftsman. He is
currently a legal consultant with the Government of Zambia. His
family involvement with the GAA at the highest level goes back three
generations to 1884, and he has been collecting data for this study of
Cusack for over two decades, during the course of which he discovered
a file of Cusack's long-forgotten newspaper, *The Celtic Times*.

Marcus de Búrca

Michael Cusack and the GAA

ANVIL BOOKS

First published 1989
Anvil Books
45 Palmerston Road, Dublin 6

ISBN   0 947962 49 2

Origination by Computertype Ltd.
Printed in Ireland by Mount Salus Press

CONTENTS

ABBREVIATIONS

AAA:	Amateur Athletic Association (of England)
AAAI:	Amateur Athletic Association of Ireland
CT:	*Celtic Times*
DAC:	Dublin Athletic Club
DAAC:	Dublin Amateur Athletic Club
DHC:	Dublin Hurling Club
FJ:	*Freeman's Journal*
GAA:	Gaelic Athletic Association
GU:	Gaelic Union
ICA:	Irish Cyclists Association
ICAC:	Irish Champion Athletic Club
INL:	Irish National League
IRB:	Irish Republican Brotherhood
IS:	*Irish Sportsman*
NLI:	National Library of Ireland
PRO:	Public Record Office (now National Archive)
RIC:	Royal Irish Constabulary
SPIL:	Society for the Preservation of the Irish Language
UI:	*United Ireland*

FOREWORD

The purpose of this book is to bring together, mainly for followers of Gaelic games but also for anybody interested in the life of the founder of the GAA, the relatively scant amount of information that has survived about Michael Cusack. Principally, I have tried to explain how and why he founded the GAA, and how and why, after only twenty months, the GAA removed him from his post as Secretary. To a lesser extent, I have also tried to give some account of his early career and to assess his later minor role in the GAA.

I am indebted to many people for information supplied and collected. Amongst those to whom a special word of thanks is due are Brother Liam P. O Caithnia, Ms Pat O'Connell (UCG Library), Des Crowe and Séan Ryan of the Clare GAA Board, Frank Burke of the Galway GAA Board, Father P. O Laoi of Co. Clare and Fathers M. Coen and J. Shiel of Co. Galway, and Prof. R. Ely of the University of Tasmania. I am especially grateful to the owner of the file of Cusack's paper *Celtic Times* for giving me access to it — and for donating his file to the Clare County Library in the month in which this book appeared.

Both the Central Council of the GAA and the Clare County Committee of the GAA have provided generous grants towards the cost of publication of this book.

Marcus de Búrca,
November 1989

The Cusack homestead, Carron, Co. Clare

CHAPTER ONE

A BURREN BOYHOOD

1847–1866

Less is known about the early life of Michael Cusack, the founder of the GAA, than about that of any other important figure in modern Irish history. When he died in 1906 Cusack was in his sixtieth year; yet all that is known with certainty about how he spent his first thirty years could probably be told in a dozen sentences. Not until he settled permanently in Dublin some months before his thirtieth birthday did Cusack become a person about whose activities solid evidence can be collected a century later. Then, after about fifteen eventful years, he retreated frustratingly into the shadows of semi-anonymous suburban existence for the last sixteen years of his life, emerging only briefly now and again.

Born on 20 September 1847 in the parish of Carron on the eastern fringe of the remote Burren area of north Clare, Michael Cusack was one of five children of Matthew Cusack and Bridget Flannery. His only sister, Mary, was three years older than Michael, and he had three brothers — John (who was older than Michael), and Patrick and Thomas, born in 1852 and 1853 respectively. Neither parent, it would seem, was from Carron. Matthew Cusack almost certainly came from Rath near Corofin, some eight miles to the south of Carron, and his wife probably from the Ennis area, about eight miles further south again. Her family burial-plot was in Drumcliffe cemetery on the edge of that town.

One of the great natural curiosities of this country, the Burren contains mineralogical and vegetational features found nowhere else on this island. An area of some fifty square miles lying generally north of the spa resort of Lisdoonvarna, it presents one of the strangest landscapes of Western Europe. It comprises mainly a vast dry almost treeless plateau of bleached limestone, shaped by millions of years of rain and wind into enormous stone terraces. In the sheltered crevices of these giant rock pavements, tiny brilliantly coloured plants, normally found only in the warm climate of southern Europe, thrive in profusion in the uncertain heat of an Irish summer.

As this enormous plateau gradually descends westwards towards the Atlantic Ocean it disintegrates strikingly into huge boulders of fantastic shapes and nightmare sizes. These almost suggest the existence in prehistoric times of a race of giants, a belief strongly held by no less a person than Michael Cusack himself, who retained to the end of his life a strong sentimental attachment to his native area.[1] This theory, it has to be conceded, is strengthened by an abundance of archaeological remains all over the Burren dating from pre-Christian times. They include stone circles, megalithic tombs and no less than 700 stone forts.

As is well known, the great majority of the people of rural Ireland at the time of the Great Famine of the late 1840s had to endure appallingly low living standards. High rents, over-crowding caused by over-population, subsistence farming, low agricultural productivity, woefully inadequate incomes and subhuman housing conditions were all common features of life for the small farmer or farm-labourer of the time, even in areas where the quality of farmland was good. How much harsher life must have been in the inhospitable and seemingly barren hills and valleys of north Clare is not difficult to imagine even today. To the visitor accustomed to the fertile countryside of Leinster or the Golden Vale it is a mystery how, even in this age of state and EEC aids to agriculture, the farmers of the Burren manage to earn a reasonable living.

Just how hard life in Clare in the early decades of the nineteenth century was may be gauged from the fact that, long before the mid-1840s, famine was no stranger there. In 1822, when typhus struck the county so many died that uncoffined burials were resorted to; in 1830, a shortage of potatoes again caused great hardship in Clare. Further outbreaks of typhus occurred in 1840 and 1845; in 1842, a general shortage of food led to riots. So bad was the famine of 1846 in Clare that employment in public works was barred to those known to be able to secure one meal a day. Two years later sixty-two persons died in Kilrush workhouse in one January week, and by May 1848 the dreaded potato blight was widespread in Clare.

For several reasons the Famine hit hardest in the counties along the western seacoast. Because the land there was so poor, living conditions were already worse than in the rest of the country. Furthermore, the people of the western counties were almost totally dependent on the potato as their principal food; so, when widespread blight occurred, it brought even more disastrous consequences than elsewhere. In addition, Clare was one of the areas where the incidence of the dreaded famine (or relapsing) fever was noticeably higher than elsewhere.

Understandably, a remote district like the Burren did not escape the impact of the Famine; indeed, it seems that its very remoteness made the impact all the more severe. Official observers noticed a greater reluctance in this part of the country to seek refuge in the dreaded workhouse until an advanced stage of starvation had been reached. Because of this, the Burren was described in November 1847 (only weeks after Cusack was born) as a nest of filth, famine and disease. Fear of infection had made the traditional funeral wake almost extinct, funerals being attended only by the number of relatives required to carry the corpse to the grave.

Since the effect of the Famine period was felt for many years, it is not surprising that the rate of emigration from Clare continued to be unusually high in the 1850s and 1860s. Between 1841 and 1851, the population fell by nearly 74,000, or 25%. While the annual average for the '50s was only 5,000, the total for the year 1851 was over 16,000, and for 1852 and 1853 over 8,000 each year. For the period from 1861 to 1869, some 32,000 people left Clare, and although in 1868 the total fell to 1,600 it rose to over 5,500 for 1864. All through the 1860s more women emigrated than men. Amongst the female emigrants from Clare in 1864 was Cusack's sister Mary.[2] She settled in Australia, as, later in the 1860s, did several Corofin Cusacks who were almost certainly cousins of Mary. So in all probability did her oldest brother John.

The parish of Carron, according to an account published in 1837, was 'chiefly rocky pasture well adapted for sheep, of which the farmers' stock principally consists'.[3] Although at different times his children described him differently, according to local tradition Michael Cusack's father Matthew was a shepherd. This in mid-nineteenth century Clare usually meant a tenant-manager of a tract of sheep pasture. In return for managing his landlord's flock the herdsman got a free residence and a small plot for his own grazing and tillage — or for both, if he was energetic enough. The 1851 census found over 900 herdspeople in Clare (over fifty of them, surprisingly, females); of these 900, one in six was under fifteen years of age. So it seems possible that Matthew Cusack had left his native Corofin for the Burren in his mid or late teens.

Today a century-and-a-half later, the Cusack homestead, which was inhabited up to 1950, still survives. Snugly fitted into a small natural saucer 150 or so yards in from the road from Corofin at

Poulaphuca, and almost hidden from sight by a sheltering copse of hazel trees, it is a surprisingly solid stone structure with three main rooms, dating from a time when roughly half of all Clare dwellings were one-roomed mud-cabins. Nearby stand a couple of outbuildings of uncertain age; in the front yard is an ageless supply of natural water. It requires little imagination to visualise the Cusacks eking out a frugal, but hardly a comfortable, existence from such a holding — assuming that Matthew Cusack possessed only some of the characteristics that his son Michael, born in 'Black '47', displayed in the second half of the century, among them a strong tenacity of purpose and great physical stamina.

About his childhood Cusack told almost nothing in later life, so little that one wonders if perhaps it was a period he did not care to remember. Both his parents were, after all, to die comparatively young, his mother at the age of forty-two of bronchitis, his father in his fifty-sixth year of pleuro-pneumonia.

In later life, Michael Cusack's recollections were of being confirmed (in July 1860), of there being no Protestants in his parish (a fact observed by Lewis in 1837), of fishing for trout and of bird-nesting, of digging potatoes for breakfast in his early teens, and of helping his father to light the annual St John's Eve bonfire from a hill near his home.[4] Beyond these trival memories of childhood, practically nothing has come from Cusack. One has to assume, for example, that because in later life he showed a knowledge of swimming he must have been swimming from boyhood.

A few more facts about his years in Carron are known that Cusack himself did not directly supply. One who seems to have been a close acquaintance half a century later claimed that Cusack was familiar with the output of the great Munster poets of two centuries before.[5] Predictably, *The Midnight Court* by the Claresman Brian Merriman was one of his favourites; he seems to have memorised many of its 1,100-odd lines. As a youth in the Burren he picked up also the traditional tales of Fionn Mac Cumhaill and the Fianna, and doubtless more recent stories about the horrors of the Famine years.

However, even in such harsh surroundings life had its lighter moments; indeed, it was often in remote areas like the Burren that the traditional pastimes of rural Ireland proved to be most resilient. On Sundays after Mass, probably the only occasion each week when the 130-odd families in the parish met, Cusack with the other boys of Carron hurled and took part in athletics — running, jumping and weight-throwing ('casting a stone').[6] From the number of outstanding athletes, quite disproportionate to its population, that Clare produced in the second half of the last century (among them Cusack himself) it is obvious that these three forms of athletic pursuits were widely engaged in at adult level in the two decades after the Famine. Moreover, jumping and weight-throwing in their several variations came to be regarded later by Cusack as so peculiarly Irish that he came to refer to them, somewhat provocatively, as 'pure athletics'.

Recent research has shown that hurling too survived the Famine in Clare, and only became more or less extinct in that county perhaps as late as thirty years after the Famine, that is, shortly before the foundation of the GAA in 1884. We have it from Cusack not only that he hurled as a boy of fifteen after Mass in Carron, but also by clear implication that he had been hurling from infancy. In 1883, he wrote that he had played the game in many forms and under many conditions — with goals a mile apart; across fields and walls; in a room; in snow and in intense heat.[7]

In addition to being reared in surroundings in which much of the traditional pre-Famine life-style had been retained, Michael Cusack grew up in a home and in an area where Irish was still the language of daily life. Indeed, it is very likely that he was eleven years old by the time he first used English or even heard it widely used — in the newly opened local national school. He quickly came to acquire a complete mastery of English, and to the end of his life remained genuinely bilingual. According to the 1851 census, over 85% of the population of the barony of Burren spoke Irish — compared to 60% for Clare as a whole and 44% for Munster.

2

About Cusack's early education we are partly in the dark, and seem destined to remain so in spite of some official records. The mystery concerns where he received his first schooling, for perhaps three or four years before Carron national school opened its doors in November or December 1858. When Lewis visited Carron in 1836 or 1837 he found two pay-schools with 150 children on the rolls; but it seems unlikely that these were still flourishing in the mid-1850s. Equally unlikely, given the travel conditions in Clare at that time, is the possibility that a boy of his years would have been sent to Corofin national school eight miles off, where he would have had some cousins for company. According to the parish priest of Carron in 1856, Father James Gleeson, the Carron children either could not or would not travel four miles to the nearest school at Glencolmcille.[8]

A possibility that cannot be ruled out, in an area like the Burren then apparently badly served by normal schools, is that Cusack first attended a hedge school, and that it was there he learned about the Munster poets and the sagas of the Fianna. Although the introduction of the national school system in 1830s sounded the death-knell of the hedge schools, they lingered on until the legislation of 1878 setting up the intermediate education system.[9] Official records show that in the late 1850s there were at least two hedge schools in Kilnaboy near Corofin, and two more near Lough Cutra in the Clare-Galway border in the mid-1860s.[10] One may assume that at least one hedge school flourished in the Carron district when Cusack was of school-going age; that he never claimed having attended one proves nothing, since he recorded practically nothing about his early education.

What we can state with near certainty about Cusack's early education is that he must have enrolled in Carron national school from shortly after it opened its doors early in November or December 1858, and that he must have been a bright pupil.[11] Both these assumptions are based on the known fact that in March 1862, little more than three years after the school opened, Cusack was made a senior monitor there.[12] A monitor was a better-than-average senior pupil who was selected to help the teacher for portion of each day, so that this is the first evidence we have — at the age of fifteen — of Cusack's general intelligence and ability.

Moreover, in the normal course of events a monitor was selected as such because his teacher considered him to be suitable material for training later as a teacher. Once a monitor attained the age of eighteen he could apply for training at a model school. In Cusack's case we also know that he was well above average as a monitor. According to the local District Inspector, one A.S. Cowley, Michael Cusack was 'the most promising monitor in the district', meaning, one can safely assume, at least the whole of Clare, since there were only thirty-seven District Inspectors of Cowley's grade for the whole thirty-two counties.[13]

Of course, some at least of the credit for turning out such good material must go to Cusack's teacher in Carron. The first principal there was Thomas Finn, who had qualified in 1852 at the age of twenty-three and transferred to Carron from Gortaclare school, also in the Burren.[14] In his early years in Carron, Finn had his problems with the inspectorate — or it with him, depending on one's prejudice. However, eventually he settled down to become a competent principal, and by the time Cusack became his senior monitor the Commissioners of National Education were satisfied with the job Finn was doing.[15]

In later life Cusack proved to be a successful, even gifted, teacher at three levels — as a national teacher, as a secondary teacher and as the principal of an academy which prepared men for entry to the universities and to the public service. That he had a flair for teaching became apparent to Finn or Cowley (or both) when he was still a monitor because, although the normal monitoring term was three years, in November 1864, after only two-and-a-half years, Cusack (then only seventeen) got a place as a pupil teacher in the District Model School in Enniscorthy, Co. Wexford.

The year 1864 was also one that Michael Cusack would remember for two other reasons of a personal or family nature. In May his mother died of bronchitis at an age when her two youngest boys Thomas and Patrick were still only eleven and twelve years old. That same year her daughter Mary, then twenty, emigrated to Australia, where she died as recently as 1929. Since it is likely that the eldest son John had preceded Mary to Australia, the departure from home (permanently, as it was to prove) of Michael in 1864 reduced the Cusack family in Clare from six to three in one year.

Apart from a few visits back to it near the end of his life, Michael Cusack was to spend only another eight months of his life in Clare after 1864. For this reason, before following his fortunes elsewhere it is, perhaps, worth considering how his boyhood in the Burren influenced his outlook, character and personality. It hardly needs to be said that to his early surroundings and experience of life in Clare he owed his love of the language of his home, his knowledge of and pride in the literature of that tongue and, not least, his lifelong attachment to his native county.

In addition, to his formative years in Clare may be traced Cusack's lifelong sympathy for the downtrodden and his sense of injustice at the plight of the ordinary people down the centuries. At a time when such views were not popular — indeed, were widely regarded as radical — these characteristics later made Cusack in a certain sense an ardent egalitarian, even a socialist in outlook. Understandably, he came to ascribe the poverty of his country and its people to British rule, to which he remained implacably opposed all his life. Over forty-one years later, within months of his death, he was still complaining bitterly of the 'miserable, degrading, crushing, bruising social system', which worked against 'the natural pleasurableness of life'.[16]

For modern Irish history and modern Irish sport, of course, no trait that he carried with him from his boyhood in Clare was to be more lasting in its effects than Cusack's love of athletics and of the national ball-game of hurling, a love which began in the Burren. It was there he was introduced to both types of traditional outdoor pastimes, and while he seems to have practised athletics regularly, after leaving Clare it was his latent love of hurling, coupled with a desire to see athletics opened to all, that eventually led to his decision to found the GAA.

Established in 1831, the national school system was an attempt by Britain to control the elementary education of every Irish boy and girl and thereby to foster a great degree of loyalty to British rule. However, because it envisaged a secular or non-denominational education, the system met with the opposition of the Catholic Church from the start. Indeed, much sooner and much clearer than nationalist opinion of the time did, the Catholic bishops saw the dangers which the spread of the national schools would bring to the already decaying separate Irish cultural identity.

In time a substantial minority of Catholic bishops and clergy came to adopt a more compromising and less rigid attitude, once they realised that they could turn the new schools to their own advantage. However, while power-sharing at local or parish level made many Catholic clerics live with the system, any degree of Catholic control over either the central model school in Dublin or the several district model schools scattered throughout the provinces was out of the question. Accordingly, these institutions incurred particularly bitter hostility from the Catholic Church — again, it needs to be stressed, with many individual or local exceptions.

Nevertheless, even the episcopal disapproval of the model schools did not prevent some Catholic trainees from attending them, in breach of an episcopal ban imposed in 1862. One such exception was Michael Cusack, who proceeded in the three years after he left home in November 1864 to break with impunity one rule after another of the new educational system. To say he did so with impunity is indeed to understate, for with each apparent breach of the rules he actually bettered himself.

For a start, Cusack remained in attendance as a pupil teacher at the District Model School at Enniscorthy for a whole year — from November 1864 to November 1865 — at a time when the normal period of attendance was only six months. Of the nature of the instruction he received at Enniscorthy we know practically nothing. It is clear that the regime there was strict. Private tuition by pupil teachers was forbidden; serious misconduct such as over-indulgence in alcohol was severely punished; good conduct was rewarded by monetary gratuities.[17]

It is safe to assume, however, that a high standard of instruction was achieved by the model schools, and his later success leads one to believe that Cusack's year in Enniscorthy was well spent. If one excludes a later period of self-instruction, about which we also know next to nothing, his year in Enniscorthy was the only substantial period of formal education Cusack spent after leaving Carron national school. Moreover, it is clear from the post he took up when he left Enniscorthy that all concerned felt he was well fitted for it.

By a happy coincidence — if indeed it was a coincidence at all — just as Michael Cusack finished a year in Enniscorthy, the permanent teacher at Richmond national school in Corofin left to do his final training in Dublin. Cusack took his place, so getting his first teaching post not merely in his native county but in what he, somewhat inaccurately but sentimentally, called 'my native parish'.

Understandably, since it served a town, Richmond was a much bigger school than that at Carron. It actually pre-dated the national school system, and in 1865-66 its average attendance was 100, double that on the Carron roll-book.[18] Because of its proximity to his home and also because it is safe to assume that at seventeen Cusack was already a prodigious walker, it can be taken for granted that while teaching at Richmond school he resided in Carron. Once again Cusack seems to have broken the rules, for although the Commissioners of National Education required a newly qualified teacher to remain two years in his (or her) first school, Cusack was gone from Richmond "by the middle of 1866', to quote himself.

'The second half of the year 1866 found me in training as a schoolmaster in Dublin,' Cusack recalled in February 1896. This is all we have from him about his first stay in a city in which some eleven years later he was to settle permanently. Since the Central Model School was located in Marlborough Street (now Department of Education offices) just off O'Connell (then Sackville) Street, he must have lodged somewhere in the north-central area, where he came to reside permanently from 1877.

To Cusack, Dublin in 1866 must have seemed a strange, almost alien, place, filled with unmistakeable political tensions. The disaffection which had found expression in the Fenian movement was still smouldering just beneath the surface. In spite of the British Government offensive against the Fenians in the previous year — the suppression of its weekly organ, *The Irish People,* and the arrest, trial, conviction and imprisonment of most of the Fenian leaders — popular sympathy with the Fenian organisation was still widespread. In Dublin city in particular there was strong support for the underground republican body.

Nowhere, indeed, was the evidence of Government unease about the Fenians more noticeable than in this city. Troops that had been rushed across from Britain were to be seen regularly patrolling the streets. On roadside hoardings a reward of £2,000 (some £200,000 by the values of 120 years later) was offered for James Stephens, the escaped Fenian leader still at large. Substantial hoards of arms continued to be found in nationalist homes, and the less well-off made no secret of their republican sympathies.

In such circumstances prudence would have ensured that a youth of Cusack's age, sympathies and background, about to qualify for a profession under official auspices, would have kept a low profile in the Dublin of late 1866. If, as seems likely, he worked hard at his final studies he did the wise thing. Furthermore, if there was any mid-summer break at the Central Model School it may be that his first stay in Dublin lasted even less than six months.

However, it seems that the wide-awake Clare youth remained by no means aloof from life in the several educational establishments housed in the Marlborough Street buildings opposite the Catholic pro-cathedral. He picked up enough information about the Resident Commissioner of National Education, Mr (later Sir) Patrick Keenan to come to dislike the man intensely, and to challenge openly nearly twenty years later Keenan's good faith and competency on Irish education. He also got to know enough about the famous historian P.W. Joyce, then headmaster of the male model school, to be able to criticise him publicly in the mid-1880s for his apathy towards the Irish language.[19]

That Cusack did in fact apply himself diligently to his studies while in Dublin is clear from the results he achieved in

Marlborough Street. For when professors Robert Sullivan and Edward Butler came to mark the examination papers for 1866 the records show that they awarded Michael Cusack the classification which he later proudly described as 'first [division] of second [class] — the highest possibly attainable at the time for a man or boy of my age and experience.' The eighteen-year-old herdsman's son from the Burren had found his vocation in life.

Footnotes

1. *Shamrock,* Vol. 20, pp. 631 & 663.
2. Death certificate of Mary Cusack (Australia).
3. Samuel Lewis, *Topographical Dictionary of Ireland* (London, 1837), Vol. 1, p. 282.
4. *Nation,* 20.7.1889 & 5.10.1889; *Shamrock,* Vol. 20, p. 191; do., 5.8.1882; CT, 18.6.1887.
5. P.J. Devlin ('Celt') in *Gaelic Football,* ed. Carbery (Dublin, 1941).
6. *Nation,* 20.7.1889.
7. *Shamrock,* Vol. 20, p. 367.
8. PRO, 2C-66-80, Folio 179.
9. P.J. Dowling, *The Hedge Schools of Ireland* (Cork, 1935), p. 153.
10. PRO, 2C-66-80, Folio 175; 2C-67-18, p. 12a.
11. PRO, 2C-56-39, Folio 11.
12. ibid.
13. PRO, 2C-67-18, p. 12a; *Thom's Directory,* 1867, p. 876.
14. PRO, 2C-66-80, Folio 166.
15. PRO, 2C-56-39, Folio 11.
16. *Clare Champion,* 10.2.1906.
17. PRO, 2C-54-4, Folio 49.
18. PRO, 2C-56-38; ibid, 2C-66-80, Folio 166.
19. *Nation,* 14.5.1884.

Principal Sources

Census of Ireland, 1851 and 1871.

Dal gCais, No. 5 (articles by MacMahon, pp. 89-93, and O Tuathaigh, pp. 110-114).

Margaret Cusack prayer-book (entries) 1880; property of Miss P. O'Connell, U.C.G.

Michael Cusack letter (Candlemas Day 1896) to J. Costello; copy in *Irish Independent* GAA Golden Jubilee Supplement, Easter 1934.

Midland Tribune, 9.3.1901.

Carron National School roll-book (in possession of Carron P.P.).

Records of births, marriages and deaths, Joyce House, Dublin 2.

R. Dudley Edwards and T.D. Williams (ed), *The Great Famine* (Dublin, 1956).

D.H. Akenson, *The Irish Education Experiment* (London, 1970).

Annual Register, 1866.

CHAPTER TWO

TEACHING IN FOUR PROVINCES
1867-1877

On New Year's Day 1867, Lord Gough of Lough Cutra Castle near Gort in Co Galway opened a new national school at Lough Cutra exclusively for sons of his tenants. The headmaster of this new school was Michael Cusack, who had been appointed to the post on the last day of 1866 and had probably spent Christmas at home with his widowed father and two younger brothers.

Although he was to spend five years there, once again Cusack himself supplied the minimum of information about his stay at Lough Cutra — merely his dates of arrival and departure and his teaching grade. Fortunately, however, in this case, probably because of the unusual nature of the school, a small amount of background information which has survived enables one to get some idea of Cusack's life for the next five years or so.

Situated some four miles south of the town of Gort, Lough Cutra is a large lake in pleasantly wooded and low hilly country in the extreme south-west corner of Galway, adjoining north-east Clare. In the 1860s the area was thickly populated by tenant-farmers who had lobbied the Commissioners of National Education for a school. For educating its children this community had been dependent on two hedge-schools. One was two miles away and the other had closed down in the mid-1860s; the nearest conventional school was about twelve miles away.

In November 1865, the landlord Gough submitted plans for a school to the authorities, and a year later the fine cut-stone slated building (which still survives), erected entirely at his own expense, was ready. He would, Gough stated in a later application for financial aid towards the teachers' salaries and other expenses, be its patron, manager and correspondent. The report on Gough's application, by none other than District Inspector Cowley, was wholly favourable of the new teacher, the prospects of the new venture succeeding, the genuinely non-denominational nature of the school, the arrangements for pupils' fees and so on.

About the religious aspect of the new school, Cowley was both

Lough Cutra School, Gort

optimistic and realistic. In 1865, the sympathetic local parish priest (of Beagh), Father John Barry, had forecast a good attendance at the proposed new school. Now in 1867 he told Cowley in the presence of Father Timothy Shannon, parish priest of Gort and vicar general of the then united dioceses of Kilmacduagh and Kilfenora, that he had no objection to the school. However, in a revealing qualification reflecting the hierarchy's policy, he indicated that he could not openly support it without a share in the management. Nevertheless, it appears from Cowley that the parents were satisfied with the plan, then common in such circumstances, to devote the last period of the afternoon to religious instruction. One suspects that it also satisfied Father Barry.

However, Bishop MacEvilly of Galway, destined to succeed the great Archbishop McHale at Tuam, took a somewhat sterner line on the Lough Cutra project. Regarding Father Barry as 'a rather simple kind of man' because he 'did not see any harm in Protestant control', the bishop 'took a different view', with which he lost no time in acquainting Gough. 'I wrote the P.P. a long elaborate letter ... which he forwarded to ... Gough ... Although polite and complimentary ... I hinted that ... if necessary we would build another school..'[1]

Lord Gough, with his new school now erected, his teacher installed and his tenants ready to send their sons to his school, was presumably not anxious for a confrontation with his Catholic tenantry or its clergy. He at once capitulated to the bishop, who (without any grounds that are apparent all these years later for such a suspicion) apparently feared lest the boys of Lough Cutra be somehow brainwashed by Gough into becoming Protestants. With Gough's agreement, Father Barry became the manager of the newly opened school, and both the staff and the textbooks were also agreed to by all concerned.

One thing that emerges from this minor skirmish between Church and State is that Michael Cusack was acceptable to all those involved on either side. That he was approved by his earlier champion Cowley, the District Inspector, is obvious; as for Gough, he apparently took his new headmaster at face value, and was possibly aware of Cowley's approval. More significant is the fact that, despite having attended two of the dreaded model schools, Cusack passed muster with bishop, vicar general and parish priest, one or more of whom must have examined his credentials carefully before making such a favourable decision.

There is every reason to believe that all concerned — the State, the Church and (not least important) the parents of the Lough Cutra boys — were more than satisfied with their new teacher. Cusack stayed almost five years, and would probably have stayed for twenty-five had he not in the meantime fitted himself for something more rewarding and more lucrative than elementary education. That he fitted into his new post at once is suggested by the fact that within four months he was allowed (again presumably with Cowley's support) to select his own unpaid monitor.

Before the school at Lough Cutra had opened Lord Gough had enrolled fifty boys, all sons of local farmers; Cowley forecast an average of fifty-one. Two inspections in January and February of 1867 showed an average daily attendance of forty-four (eighty-eight per cent), which fell to thirty-seven at a third inspection the following October. By 1869 the daily average had risen to fifty-five. Cusack's starting salary was £18 a year. By charging weekly fees of one, two or three pennies depending on the age of the pupils, Gough guaranteed to bring this figure to £44 until proof of Cusack's grade came through. When it did, the £18 was increased to £32.

Although no record of what subjects Cusack taught at Lough Cutra has survived, it is safe to assume that he confined himself to the three fundamental subjects of reading, writing and arithmetic. In view of his lifelong expertise in every aspect of the English language, and as he would have had no illusions about its importance to any boys who would not spend their adult lives in the area, one may surmise that he put special emphasis on this particular subject. The religious instruction appears also to have been given by Cusack, a fairly common practice in those days and one that is understandable in this case in view of Cusack's approval by the Church.

Very little has survived in the official records about what the Commissioners of National Education thought of Cusack while he was at Lough Cutra. But that little suggests that the inspectorate found him suitable in every way. His 'acquirements, character and method of conducting school' were all commented on favourably. On the negative side, he appears not to have merited attention for any of the faults such as incompetency, inaccurate accounts or addiction to drink that are scattered throughout the early records of the national school system.

What, one may wonder at this point, did Michael Cusack think of this new educational system under which, by the time he left Cutra, he had spent one-third of his life as an unpaid or paid servant? To answer this question one need go no further than a series of letters by Cusack in a nationalist paper in 1884, when he mounted a blistering attack on one of the National Education Commissioners over a period of four months. Clearly the views he expressed then, if not actually formed when at Lough Cutra fifteen years before, were obviously based on his experience as the headmaster of Lough Cutra boys national school from 1867 to 1871.

The national school system was, in Cusack's view, 'an insufferable system'. It taught nothing of the language, literature or music of our forefathers. By not permitting the Irish language to be used as a medium of instruction in Irish-speaking areas it fulfilled the prophecy of Archbishop McHale that the national schools would become the graveyard of the Irish language.[2] Moreover, a curriculum that excluded Irish history and that had literally no time for physical pastimes (Irish or otherwise) cannot have met with the approval of Lough Cutra's first headmaster.

However, from his remarkable successes as a teacher in Dublin some ten years later, it is clear that Cusack had from the start a gift for instructing young men. One can be sure that within the limitations imposed on him by the system he did an excellent job with the boys of south Galway. Furthermore, initially at any rate he thought sufficiently well of the system to take on in March 1867 as an unpaid senior monitor one Thomas Cusack, who was almost certainly his own fourteen-year-old brother, recently left Carron national school. Thomas was promised the princely salary of £6 a year from 1868, and his arrival brought his older brother an annual training allowance of fifteen shillings — 75p in 1989 terms.

Of Cusack's private life at Lough Cutra we know almost nothing, and nearly all of it from sources other than himself. Although Gough had built separate teachers' residences — one for the master and one for the mistress — they may not have been completed when Cusack arrived. A tradition in Gort insists that he lodged in that town, presumably making the four-mile journey on foot five mornings a week (and back again each afternoon) — a practice he could hardly have continued for long. Reliable tradition in Gort also insists that he became a close friend of Dan Burke and Ned Treston, both of whom are said to have been enthusiastic supporters of Irish games.

From Gort too comes an almost incredible story — that on Friday evenings when school closed for the week-end Cusack set off on foot on the twelve-mile journey to Carron, another feat he hardly kept up during the winter months. Indeed, one of only two references by him to Gort shows that in 1870 he attended a public meeting in the town square, relating to some local agitation and probably held at a week-end.[3]

One week-end that Cusack almost certainly spent in his native area was the first week-end of March 1867, when the abortive Fenian Rising took place. Although one is totally dependent on oral tradition, it seems certain that in or near the town of Corofin a large crowd (probably running into four figures) of local young men assembled on the night of 3-4 March; but, without a proper leadership and poorly equipped, they dispersed before dawn. A local priest named McMahon is credited with having been sympathetic to the Fenian cause, and (as is know to have happened elsewhere) it may have been he who prudently persuaded the force to give up what would have been a foolhardy attempt to capture the local police barracks.

A high proportion of the young men in the Corofin district are believed to have been sworn into the Fenian organisation and, although we have only his own word for it, it seems likely that amongst those who assembled under cover of darkness was the twenty-year-old Michael Cusack — who risked instant dismissal as a teacher for his action. It was to be twenty years before Cusack first publicly referred to the event, but four statements he made between 1895 and 1901 leave one in little doubt that he had been a Fenian in 1867. Acquaintances of Cusack around the turn of the century, as varied as James Joyce and the GAA writer P.J. Devlin ('Celt'), were satisfied about his connection with the early Fenian movement.[4]

Significantly, probably the clearest memory of him that survived into the present century concerned his athletic prowess. He was remembered as 'a great athlete', being particularly good at the high jump. Specifically, it was recalled that he was able to clear a five-foot gate in a local avenue almost from a standing position, something none of the local high-jumpers could do — a feat that doubtless enabled Cusack to boast of the superiority of Claremen.[5] It seems likely that it was on the lake at Lough Cutra that Cusack acquired the knowledge of rowing that he showed when he settled in Dublin in 1874.

That he also played bowls — the ancient pastime that now survives only on secondary roads of Armagh and Cork — while at Lough Cutra seems likely; in 1885 he recalled the prowess of the young and middle-aged bowlers on the roads of that area fifteen years before.[6] Understandably, because the game was not then played around Lough Cutra, there is no local tradition of his playing hurling there. However, when the local men played football in a field known as "an péac rua", which is directly opposite the school, Cusack joined in.

One may ask next how such a mentally active young man, as we known from his later life that Cusack was, filled the long winter evenings for nearly five years in a remote place like Lough Cutra, with the nearest town over four miles away. As already suggested, because of the primitive road conditions then common in such areas one may assume that he could not regularly have walked home to Carron at week-ends once winter set in. His later career in secondary education surely provides the answer: he studied in his spare time in order to advance beyond primary teaching. Furthermore, since his father had died in July 1868, Cusack's visits to Carron probably became less frequent from then on.

One thing is certain. His change in 1871 from being the headmaster of an obscure rural elementary school to the position of professor in an old-established Catholic seminary-cum-secondary school, at least 150 miles away at the other end of the country, was not a sudden change. Admittedly, local tradition ascribes the actual timing of his move to a worsening in his personal relations with Lord Gough, who apparently became increasingly irritated by his teacher's fraternising with the local community. Nevertheless, the evidence forces one to the conclusion that Cusack's departure was the result of a deliberate decision that he must have made a couple of years earlier, one that necessitated the acquisition of the necessary professional qualification to obtain employment as a secondary teacher.

Exactly what that extra qualification was cannot be stated with certainty all these years later. What is known is that Micheal Cusack was by no means the only national teacher who by self-education in his spare time lifted himself out of primary teaching into better-paid positions, mostly in the young but expanding Irish, English and Indian civil services. Furthermore, because of the nature of two at least of the four teaching posts Cusack held in the early 1870s, it is reasonably clear that the new qualification he had by then acquired involved the two subjects of commerce and accountancy, and probably also a higher standard of both English and mathematics then that obtainable by trainees at the national teachers' training schools.

2

By the summer of 1871, it seems safe to assume, Michael Cusack had equipped himself for a post as a secondary teacher. By early October at the latest he had got such a post, and in mid-October he resigned his position at Lough Cutra. Three days later, on 16 October 1871, he arrived in Newry in Co Armagh, where he had been appointed Professor of English and Mathematics in St Colman's College. He was to stay there almost three years.[7]

Violet Hill, as St Colman's was locally known, was a very different institution from the boys' national school at Lough Cutra. Founded half a century earlier as the Catholic seminary for the diocese of Dromore, it had had a chequered career in its first forty-eight years. Although in its early period it had prospered under the presidency of Bishop Blake, it was obliged to suspend operations three times between 1837 and 1860, when it often had as few as a dozen (sometimes even fewer) boys on its roll-books.

Then in 1869 under a new president, Father (later Bishop) Henry O'Neill, it began a new period of modern expansion. A more practical curriculum was introduced and a decision taken to employ some lay teachers. In addition, tuition was offered to boys who did not intend to become priests. Gradually the new regime won support locally. The number of lay students began to grow, and Violet Hill began to turn out boys who became successful professional men in many parts of the country.

The English Department, of which Cusack was probably in charge, catered not only for English but also for Irish and English history, geography and mathematics, including book-keeping. It is easy to understand how this wider range of subjects would have attracted Cusack after nearly five years of frustration imposed by the restricted curriculum of the national school system. In addition, with boys of an older age-group he must have felt that he was now contributing more directly to their future than can ever have been the case with the boys at Lough Cutra.

Furthermore, it would have been natural for a sociable, not to say gregarious, personality such as we know Cusack to have been later to find his surroundings in Newry challenging and even pleasant. With a population of 13,500 in which those of the nationalist or Catholic persuasion were in the majority, Newry was a lively prosperous place, serving both as a sea-port and a market-town. One wonders indeed if it reminded Cusack of his brief stay in Dublin five years before. Perhaps this first real taste of urban life made him think again of that even bigger city sixty-five miles to the south, which he knew to be in every sense the capital of his country.

Because of his success in Dublin a few years later in building friendships with those of a different cultural, political or religious background from his own, one may surmise that he became a good mixer in Newry and enjoyed a pleasant social life. A few at least of his pupils there became lifelong friends. He seems to have explored the coastal area within reach of Newry, getting as far as Rostrevor and probably Greenore.[8]

It seems certain that it was in Newry that he first met Margaret Woods, a seventeen-year-old girl from the town of Dromore twenty miles to the north of Newry. Margaret's family were prosperous shopkeepers in Dromore and she probably had relatives in Newry;

Margaret Cusack

her father James had died in 1869. Indeed, she may well have been employed at St Colman's, where there would have been plenty of work for a seamstress, for such was her occupation.

Once again one is driven to speculation about Cusack, for the simple reason that once again he himself told us nothing — beyond the dates of arrival and departure — about the two-and-a-half years he spent in Newry. How he obtained the Violet Hill post, how he got on in St Colman's or in the Newry area, and finally why he left it in the summer of 1874 all remain a mystery. 'After a month with my brother in Glamorganshire [in south Wales] I turned up at . . . Blackrock' [in Dublin], he wrote over twenty years later.

Founded in 1860 by a group of French priests, Blackrock College, known in its early years as the French College, was a success almost from the start. In 1869, 1872 and again in 1875, substantial extensions were added to the original buildings, the last involving the demolition of the whole of the once picturesque little seaside village of Williamstown. In 1875, the French College affiliated to the Catholic University. By the time Michael Cusack joined the growing lay staff, probably in the autumn of 1874, the college had almost 200 pupils, the majority of them boarders but with a handful of day-boys from local well-to-do homes.

In 1871, sixteen years after the establishment of the Civil Service Commission to regulate entry to the public service, competitive examinations became the normal method of recruitment to the service. A number of 'grinding' schools immediately opened in Dublin where pupils were specially prepared for the civil service entry tests. However, all these schools were in Protestant ownership and catered mostly for Protestant boys. Accordingly, about 1872 Blackrock College began to plan to open a Civil Service Department. Here boys would be prepared for the Irish civil service and those of Britain and India, as well as for entry to third-level institutions like the College of Surgeons in Dublin and also for the army, navy and police, all three of which had a cadet system.

One summer's day in 1874, while travelling back from the south by train, Cusack struck up a conversation with a fellow-passenger John Quinn, whose father Martin, a graduate of Galway university, had recently joined the Blackrock staff. From the younger Quinn, Cusack learned that there were vacancies for teachers of commercial subjects in the proposed new department. Expressing an interest in such a post, he accepted an invitation to stay with the Quinns at No. 1 Westfield Terrace in Williamstown, beside the college.

Although the Quinns were put off by Cusack's manner, mode of dress (including his hobnailed boots) and his drinking habits, they were mistaken in their belief that he would not be acceptable to the French fathers. Inside a fortnight he had obtained a post in Blackrock, largely it seems through the influence of Martin Quinn.

Although, for a school whose history is so well documented, surprisingly little in the form of solid facts has been recorded about Cusack's period at Blackrock, there is just about enough to give some idea of his life there from late 1874 to the end of 1875. Indeed, it is from his Blackrock days that we begin at last to get at least an outline of the personality of this complex but talented figure, who was soon to make a major impact on the sporting life of Dublin and who later still when in middle-age was to find a place in what is accepted to be the greatest novel of this century in the English language, James Joyces's *Ulysses*.

As a lay member of the staff of the Civil Service Department Cusack taught commercial subjects — presumably, book-keeping, accountancy and mathematics, and also probably English grammar or composition (or both). He lived with his pupils in the building known as the Castle, spending his whole day with them from 6 a.m. to 10 p.m. seven days a week, sharing their study hours, their meal-times and their recreation periods. Exclusive of board and lodging, his salary was £40 a year — a big improvement on his earnings at Lough Cutra.

That all this entailed a strenous, indeed exacting, routine one need not doubt. Equally clear is the fact that Cusack, who after all was still only twenty-six and thus less than ten years older than his pupils, stood up well to the rigours of life in Blackrock. He became a popular and prominent, if not a dominating, figure in this self-contained community, participating fully in its spare-time activities. Within a short time after his arrival Cusack was fully accepted by both the clerical and lay staff, who in 1875 numbered eleven laymen and six priests in the Castle. Clearly too he held his own with his professional colleagues, amongst whom was the distinguished mathematician John Casey, who later achieved world renown, who had joined Blackrock in 1873.

When, apparently for the first time in its history, Blackrock College held a St. Patrick's Day banquet on 17 March 1875, Cusack was a speaker at the function. When three months later the first College public sports were held, it was surely no coincidence that the principal events included traditional events Cusack had seen in

Clare as a boy — the hop, step and jump from a standing position, and the 16lb. and 42lb. weights.

Although no longer popular with the priests because of a recent fatality through playing it on a gravel surface, cricket (then widely played in many towns of Ireland) was still engaged in. For the first time in his life Cusack became a keen player of this distinctively English field game, even going so far as to buy a special pair of trousers for the game. When he found that the older boys, who were obliged to wear long soutanes from the age of sixteen, could not play football in their clerical garb, he devised special rules to allow for their participation. On this episode was later built the amusing but quite untenable theory that the rules of modern Gaelic football (of which Cusack was not in any event the draftsman) were framed in the college that later became a nursery of rugby football in this country.

From the start, it hardly needs to be said, Cusack not only actively encouraged but took part in every form of physical recreation engaged in at Blackrock. There, unlike St. Colman's or Lough Cutra, great emphasis was placed on this aspect of life. Special facilities were provided for gymnastics, and playing-fields were laid out in the college farm at Merrion half a mile away near Ballsbridge. In addition, as a member of several of its sports clubs, Cusack took part in outside competitions in Dublin city and its outlying suburbs and villages — as a handballer, oarsman and athlete.

Exactly why Cusack left Blackrock cannot be explained — except, perhaps, as part of a long-term plan soon to be suggested. That he was a success there as a teacher there can be no doubt. That he was happy there is also obvious; indeed, his expenditure on liquor (which included seven bottles of brandy in one month) suggests a decidedly convivial atmosphere. He made several friendships there that lasted long after he left, and seems to have acquired a proficiency in the French language from priests whose English was often imperfect. He praised the college many years later at a time when it withheld support from the body he had formed to foster Irish pastimes. He even drew into this body young men from the Blackrock area with connections in the college.

The two posts that Cusack held after that at Blackrock give, it is suggested, a clue to his reason for leaving, if one is needed at all. For three months from mid-January 1876 he was on the teaching staff of Kilkenny College, a Protestant boys' school founded as far back as 1538 by the eighth Earl of Ormonde and endowed under a charter by the Duke of Ormonde in 1684. The patrons of this venerable institution were the Board of Trinity College, Dublin, and the Marquess of Ormonde, and the visitors the Protestant Bishop of Ossory and the Provost of Trinity College.

Despite these impeccable Establishment connections, however, Kilkenny College, which numbered Jonathan Swift among its past pupils, had its ups and downs and had gone into a steep decline shortly before Cusack joined its staff. Its buildings, towards which Grattan's parliament had given a staggering grant of £5,000 (perhaps half a million pounds by today's values) back in 1782, were in a dilapidated state, and the school had to close its doors for six months in 1873. Shortly afterwards its fortunes seem to have revived when James Maxwell Weir, a Trinity graduate, became head-master. He brought with him to Kilkenny some of the pupils who had enrolled in his former school in the Crescent in Limerick city.

Once again nothing is known of Cusack's short stay in Kilkenny except his dates of arrival and departure. One naturally wonders how he fitted into this totally Protestant and loyalist atmosphere, or indeed if he fitted in at all, considering that he stayed for only one term. Was he, one wonders also, present for the annual visit by the two visitors, when according to custom teachers and pupils were entertained to a sumptuous dinner, the main course of which was a fat buck from the Earl of Ormonde's estate?

In mid-April 1876, Cusack returned to Dublin, and two months later, on 16 June, he married Margaret Woods in Dromore Catholic Church, her brother Robert being the best man.[9] Some time after this, probably in the autumn of 1876, he joined the teaching staff of Clongowes Wood College in Co Kildare; but by the summer of 1877 he had settled permanently in Dublin. There in the late autumn of that year he opened his own school.

Exactly what Cusack lived on from the time he left Kilkenny College in April 1876 to the time he arrived at Clongowes is not known. However, one need not doubt that there would have been plenty of opportunities to give private tuition in Dublin. By now he must have built up many useful connections in the teaching profession, which would have stood to him during the six months or so in the middle of 1876 when he had no steady or permanent employment.

About Cusack's period in Clongowes we know nothing either. He

*11 Emmet Street,
Dublin,
Cusack's
first home*

himself mentioned it only once, not even on that occasion giving
dates of arrival or departure, and no records of the period have
survived in the college itself.[10] As with both St Colman's in Newry
and Blackrock College, however, there is no reason to doubt that
Cusack fitted in at Clongowes. Founded in 1814 by the Jesuits,
Clongowes Wood College had long since established itself as
probably the most exclusive Catholic boys' boarding school in this
country. Amongst its pupils had been Daniel O'Connell's sons,
Thomas Francis Meagher, the Young Irelander, and the prominent
Dublin Fenian, John Flood.

The year Cusack joined the Clongowes teaching staff there was
a change of rector, Father Thomas Keating SJ succeeding Father
Robert Carbery SJ. One of Cusack's pupils was a Wexford boy,
John E. Redmond, destined to lead the Irish Parliamentary Party
at Westminster a quarter of a century later. Neither ever mentioned
the other, so far as is known. However, as at Blackrock, one may
assume that while at Clongowes Cusack participated in the various
forms of physical and mental recreation such as gravel football,
cricket, debates and walking tours of the area.

While as so often in Cusack's early life one is driven to speculation, it is not difficult to discern a pattern, indeed a definite plan, in his life from the time he learned in the summer of 1874 of the vacancy in the new Civil Service Department of Blackrock College. If the brother he visited in Wales then was Thomas, his former monitor at Lough Cutra, it is possible that the purpose of this visit was to consult him about this plan. Thomas and Michael appear to have kept in touch with one another, for Thomas was godfather to at least one of Michael's children. Whether or not he actually resigned his Newry post to join the Dublin college, it is easy to visualise him while at Blackrock gradually coming to appreciate that an opening existed for a 'grinding' academy in the city under Catholic control, competing with the existing 'civil service schools', all in Protestant hands.

One may further surmise that it was with a view to setting up his own academy in Dublin that he took both the Kilkenny and the Clongowes posts. Each would — and undoubtedly did — give him greater teaching experience, enabling him also to make contacts (both Catholic and Protestant) among staff and pupils that would be useful to him when he set up on his own. His marriage in 1876 and his acquisition or renting in 1877 of a new house in Dublin may also be seen as fitting into a plan to start his new school from his own home in the city.

Because the length of his stay at Clongowes is not known, it is impossible to state precisely when Cusack settled in Dublin. All the available evidence points to his arrival in the city early in 1877. A near-contemporary implies that Cusack did not stay long in Clongowes, and it seems likely that he had moved to the city when his first child, Clare, was born in April 1877. Emmet Street, close to Mountjoy Square, where at No. 11 he almost certainly took up residence in the first half of that year (a curious coincidence, since he was proud of the fact that he was born on the anniversary of Emmet's death) was in the course of development from 1876. Here in this new residential area, according to Cusack's own notice in several Dublin newspapers, the Civil Service Academy, of which he was the proprietor, opened in October 1877.[11]

Footnotes
1. Irish College (Rome) Archives, 1867 Carton, No. 58; MacEvilly to Kirby, 21.2.1867.
2. *Nation,* 1884; 1 March and April 26.

3. Letter Cusack to L.S. Mangan, 14.1.1900 (*recte* 1901), property of B. O Mongáin, Blackrock, Co Dublin.
4. *Irish Daily Independent,* 1.2.1895; *Shan Van Vocht* 1897 (republished in *Gaelic Athlete,* 7.3.1914); *Fainne an Lae,* 30.4.1896; *Midland Tribune,* 9.3.1901; see also, quotation in *Ellmann,* James Joyce (Oxford, 1983) at p. 459; *An Raitheachán,* March 1937 (article by 'Celt'), and *An Camán,* 1.6.1932 (anon. art.).
5. Irish Folklore Commission, Vol. 404, p. 203.
6. *UI,* 30 May 1885.
7. *Evening Herald,* 1.11.1902.
8. *Shamrock,* 21 July 1883 and 8 March 1884.
9. Dromore parish (Dromore diocese) marriage register.
10. Letter from Rev. R. Burke Savage SJ, 28.10.1981.
11. *Irishman,* 3.3.1883; *UI,* 14.7.1883; also *Gaelic American,* 15.12.1906.

Principal Sources

Cusack-Costello letter, 1896 (see Chapter 1 Sources).
R.S. Rait, *The Story of an Irish Property* (Oxford, 1908), p. 113.
PRO: 2C-67-18 (Application Book);
2C-58-71 (Salary Books, Co. Galway and Folio 69).
D.H. Akenson, *The Irish Education Experiment* (see Chapter 1 Sources).
Campbell and Mooney, *History of St. Colman's College* (Newry, 1944).
Thom's Directory, 1876, 1877, 1878.
Slaters Directory, 1870.
Belfast Directory, 1870.
Blackrock College Annual, 1954, pp. 70 and 75.
Blackrock College Annual, 1960, pp. 34-57, 68, 117, 119, 138-139.
Blackrock College Annual, 1966, pp. 73-74.
Blackrock College Annual, 1975, pp. 15-23.
W.E. Dobbs, *Notes on History of Kilkenny College 1538-1938* (Kilkenny, n.d.).
The Clongownian, 1914, pp. 14, 21, 41, 46.
The Clongowes Record, 1814 to 1932, pp. 125-126, 163.
Information supplied (1983) by Michael Keehan, Ardamullivan, Co Galway.

CHAPTER THREE

AN ATHLETIC ACADEMIC

1877–1881

The ten years starting with the opening of his own school were the most important in Cusack's life. It was then that he made the decisions and took the actions for which he deserves to be remembered in modern Irish history. To be specific, between October 1877 and November 1887 he made his mark on Irish education, played a decisive role in Irish athletics, revived the national game of hurling, took part in a seminal move to revive the Irish language, edited a new Irish weekly newspaper, and founded what has been for over a hundred years the biggest and most successful of Irish sports bodies.

So strenuous a life did Cusack lead in those ten years, and so varied were his activities, that by the end of that decade he was to a large extent a spent force. It was as if, by channelling all his energies into the several causes he took up in the 1880s, he had used up all his mental and physical resources in that period, and from then on was merely drawing on his reserves. Nothing he did in the period of almost twenty years left to him after 1887 rivalled, either in importance or in intensity of effort, anything he did in the ten years before 1887.

All this has had one unfortunate result. Until serious research into his career began in recent years, the only Michael Cusack that the Irish public has known is the composite caricature to be found in James Joyce's *Ulysses* and to a lesser extent in Oliver St John Gogarty's *Tumbling in the Hay*. What few readers of either book appreciate is that the Citizen of those two widely read novels is based on a Cusack in decline. This was a Cusack well (and sadly) past his prime, a Cusack whose faults were far more obvious than his good points, a Cusack troubled in health, beset with family troubles and worried by material matters. If one is to judge solely from their published works, neither Gogarty nor Joyce ever knew the real Michael Cusack; both were in any event too young to have known him in his prime.

However, it would be unjust to both these distinguished writers to suggest that the Cusack we meet in Joyce's and Gogarty's books is a complete distortion of the man. On the contrary, Michael Cusack did (to use the modern euphemism) have a drink problem, and was given to boasting about his achievements. He was full of prejudices of all kinds; he did have a voice of stentorian dimensions. Moreover, his dress, manner and general deportment were all of a style that invited criticism and even ridicule in late Victorian Dublin, that often intolerant, small-minded, class-ridden city that had more than its fair share of knockers.

Indeed, it seems likely that between them Joyce (in *Stephen Hero*) and Gogarty (in his chapter on the famous Dublin meeting-place known as 'An Stad') do give us brief glimpses of something approaching the real Cusack. It is a Cusack who has, perhaps, mellowed in some respects, but still a Cusack who has not modified his nationalist philosophy. At the same time it is still a very different Cusack from the Cusack of fifteen or twenty years before, when he was at the peak of his professional and public careers.

Of necessity for a newly-wed, it was his professional career that came first with Cusack immediately after his arrival in Dublin. He himself said in 1884 that for several years after his marriage he was obliged to concentrate exclusively on providing for his family. It seems likely that for some months before he opened his own school in October 1877 he had some connection, either as a partner or as merely one of the staff, with a school which had been opened in 1875 at 32 Lower Gardiner Street. The proprietor of this was one Hamilton Bell, a former national teacher who was to continue to run his own academy for another twenty-five years, and who may have taken Cusack on during the otherwise unexplained six-month period between his marriage and his probable arrival in Clongowes Wood in the autumn of 1876.

Understandably, perhaps, since it was a privately owned institution no records of Cusack's Academy (as it soon came to be known) have survived. In addition, Cusack himself has left no account of this school, which, after the GAA, was probably the most successful venture of his life. Yet, in an educational column he wrote for many years in a popular magazine, he unwittingly provided a fair amount of circumstantial evidence which enables one to give at least a general sketch of the Academy.[1]

From the start Cusack concentrated on grinding young men for the various entrance examinations for the civil services of Ireland, Britain and India. The posts he prepared his pupils for were mostly those of the lower clerical and administrative ranks of the general civil service, similar positions in the various court offices in Dublin, London and Edinburgh (many of them since abolished) and cadetships of the Royal Irish Constabulary and the British and Indian armies.

In two important respects Cusack's school (and, of course, the other grinding schools then also flourishing in Dublin) satisfied a demand in contemporary Irish post-primary education. With the national school system now almost half a century in existence, the standard of education it was providing had for several reasons (not least among these the more efficient inspection machinery) greatly improved. Yet boys unable to afford the few fee-paying secondary schools available could not adequately prepare themselves for entry to the growing number of attractive civil service posts.

Moreover, the secondary schools in general put insufficient emphasis on subjects such as commerce, accounting and even mathematics for boys intending to seek employment in the civil service or the banks. It is true that here and there, given a financial inducement (and even in some cases without that) dedicated national teachers were to be found who were prepared to give individual tuition to boys who had completed their primary schooling. Cusack himself more than once drew attention to this service, and highly praised those giving it.

Yet nobody knew better than he that many boys simply had not access to such tuition, and that at best it was but a poor substitute for the services which Cusack's and his rivals' academies were providing. Accordingly, Cusack urged boys from rural areas to come to Dublin, even though this meant having to find lodgings in the city for several months at a time, in order to be properly prepared for a competitive examination. In particular, he defended such extra expense as being preferable to paying fees for correspondence courses, which he disapproved of generally and which he felt to be totally unsuited to some important subjects.

It was ironic that it was in providing new material for the officer class of the Royal Irish Constabulary that Michael Cusack was most successful in his early years as a grinder. For his place in modern Irish history rests largely on his foundation of the GAA, which inside three years of its establishment became in the eyes of the British administration in Ireland one of the newest and most effective nationalist organisations in the country. And in monitoring the activities and progress of the GAA the RIC, as the eyes and ears of Dublin Castle, was the instrument of such surveillance.

While it was on his success in examinations for posts in the civil service and the banks that Cusack's reputation as a grinder was firmly and justifiably based, from the early 1880s onwards he extended his curriculum to cater for solicitors' apprentices preparing for Law Society tests, and from October 1883 also ran night classes for day workers. From at least 1884 onwards he gave grinds for the College of Surgeons examinations in Dublin. Finally, towards the end of the century, if one accepts that Gogarty's *Tumbling in the Hay* has at least some factual basis, it seems likely that Cusack also gave grinds to medical students generally in what might loosely be called basic non-medical subjects.

No public notice of the foundation of Cusack's Academy appears to have been published, and it was several years after it opened that Cusack began the practice of advertising his results. Two questions arise: how did he obtain his first pupils, and what were the sources of the regular intake of students in his Academy's early years? The answer to both questions can, it is suggested, be given in two words — Trinity College. There is evidence that shortly after his arrival in Blackrock College in 1874 Cusack made some acquaintances in Trinity College, participating in some of its sporting activities, with (it is suggested) as one of his motives the making of contacts that would be useful when he later opened his own school.[2]

As to how many students Cusack had on his rolls in a given year, it seems (as one might expect) that the total varied from one year to another. Naturally it was higher as the Academy prospered in the early 1880s than in its early period. In mid-1885, when under oath in the High Court, Cusack stated that between 150 and 160 of his pupils had passed their examinations since he had first opened his doors.[3] Over the seven-year period from January 1878 to January 1885, the lower figure would give twenty-one students annually; one could safely push this up to thirty to allow for failures and those who did not finish.

In ascertaining Cusack's income from his Academy there are three clues. According to the first GAA historian, T. F. O'Sullivan, who knew him well in Cusack's last few years, he was earning £1,500 a year during the Academy's most successful period.[4] Cusack himself, when in the witness-box in 1885, stated that his fee was either two guineas (£2.10) or four guineas (£4.20) per month. If an average monthly fee of three guineas (£3.15) be taken as a basis

*4 Gardiner's Place,
Dublin,
Cusack's Academy
in the 1880s*

of calculation, this produces a gross total of almost £1,150 for only thirty students. But if (as seems likely) Cusack had closer to forty students, such an average fee would produce just over £1,500 — O'Sullivan's figure. In 1883, Cusack mentioned a £10 fee for an unspecified term; if this were for three months, it would yield £1,600 annually for forty students.

Out of this gross total of around £1,500 Cusack had, of course, to meet various 'overheads' — rent, living expenses for his now growing family, and heat and light for the premises in the winter months. Understandably, as the numbers on his rolls grew (perhaps by 1880) he could no longer cope adequately on his own, and had to take on one or more teachers. How many he had on his staff cannot be stated with certainty. All we know is that they included one or more of his former colleagues from Blackrock College, Quinn among them.[5] By 1883 he also had at least one Protestant on his staff, perhaps a result of his association with Trinity and Kilkenny Colleges.

How quickly Cusack's Academy prospered is shown by the fact that a year or so after he started in Emmet Street the small single-storied house there became too small to hold both his household and his school. In 1878, he moved to 37 Nelson Street, a three-storied corner house near the Mater Hospital. By 1880 he had moved again, this time to 4 Gardiner's Place near Mountjoy Square, a handsome, spacious four-storied house now occupied by the Dergvale Hotel. Here Cusack was to remain until at least 1886; here in a real sense, rather than in Thurles, the GAA was founded.

In April 1877, around the time when, one surmises, Cusack took up residence in Emmet Street, his first child, Clare, was born. In August of the year he moved to Nelson Street (1878), his first son, Michael, was born. Thirteen months later, his second daughter, Bridget, was born, and in December 1880, some months after the move to Gardiner's Place, his second son, John (who died as recently as 1956), was born. At least three, and probably four, more children were to be born during Cusack's six years' residence at 4 Gardiner's Place.

The moves to Nelson Street and Gardiner's Place were not the only evidence of the success of Cusack's Academy. Much more convincing were his own advertisements in one or more of a half-a-dozen Dublin papers. These began to appear regularly from the early 1880s and almost invariably listed the Academy's success, usually also giving the names of the successful students. Occasionally too, Cusack was able to boast that his was the only school in Dublin to have attained a particular result.

Examples of Cusack's advertisements are easy to find. In December 1887, in his own newspaper *The Celtic Times* he announced that at the recent Customs examinations a Mr Gibney (who took first place in Dublin) and a Mr Fagan both qualified 'direct from Mr Cusack's classes'. Gibney had also been successful in a recent Excise examination. In the previous Excise examination a Mr Connor took the first place 'from the three kingdoms'; with a Mr Dolan he qualified 'direct from Mr. Cusack's classes'. Later that same month, in another notice in the same paper, Cusack announced that at the recent first open competition for junior clerkships in the High Court, Messrs Kelly and Carroll, both pupils of his Academy, had taken the two places on offer.

Perhaps the most striking evidence of Cusack's success as a

grinder is furnished by a summary of his achievements in civil service competitions published in August 1884, when his Academy was almost seven years old. Of 160 civil service successes fifty-one became temporary copyists, forty-nine Excise clerks and twenty-seven Customs officials. His Excise students included one placed first in Ireland and five placed second; his Customs students also included a first in Ireland.

Out of eight RIC cadetships four had taken first in this examination, and out of eight Land Commission clerks three had taken first place. Out of ten Class II copyists, a competition in which Cusack's was the only school in Dublin to be successful, two won first places in Ireland and three were placed second. In addition, his pupils won four boy clerkships (including one first in Ireland), one assistant-inspectorship in the Patents Office and two clerkships in the High Court, the latter the only two so far offered by open competition.

The varied social backgrounds of some of his pupils also demonstrate the high reputation attained by Cusack's Academy. According to himself boys came to him from all thirty-two counties. In one case — and there were probably others — a young man crossed specially from England to study for a particular post. Thomas St George McCarthy, a future co-founder of the GAA, left the exclusive Grammar School in Tipperary for Cusack's Academy, to prepare for the RIC cadetship test. Cusack claimed that the National Education Commissioners thought highly of him; he seems to have good sources of information in this body, and in 1882 a son of a Commissioner was a pupil of Cusack. What an even higher authority thought of Cusack is evident from the fact that the Secretary of the Royal University (predecessor of the National University), Dr David Dunne, sent his son to Cusack's.

From two very different bodies came astonishing tributes to Cusack's standing in Irish education in the early 1880s. In 1881, the reputable conservative sporting journal *The Irish Sportsman*, with whose proprietors and editorial staff Cusack's relations were always mercurial at best, devoted an entire editorial article praising the achievements of his Academy. And in 1884, a big proportion of the delegates attending the annual congress of the Irish National Teachers Organisation in Dublin attended as a body a talk Cusack gave in Irish in the Mansion House to the Gaelic Union, to show the esteem in which they held this former national teacher.

About Cusack's system or method of instruction we know very

little with certainty. However, the small size of his classes must have resulted in his pupils getting almost individual tuition — something Cusack would have become accustomed to both at Lough Cutra and Newry. While he used the then standard textbooks for subjects such as English and Mathematics, he also produced his own notes, which he had printed and sold publicly. In addition, he regularly gave homework exercises in Mathematics, Accounting and English essays, the correction of which would have obviously entailed individual attention too.

So seriously did Cusack take his vocation as a tutor of young men entrusted to his care at a formative stage of their lives that he made a point of keeping up contacts with his pupils outside class-hours. As will shortly appear, this even extended to organising their spare-time physical recreation. In the class-room itself it is clear that, while carefully avoiding imposing his own political or religious views on students, Cusack inculcated high moral standards based on broad Christian principles, and also urged patriotic sentiments.

'A nation's liberty as well as a nation's greatness depends on the education of its people, and that education must be two-fold in character — mental and physical,' wrote Cusack in 1891, when his Academy no longer flourished.[6] However, while it did flourish he certainly practised what he preached. Almost from the start he organised athletics for his pupils and in January 1882 Cusack's Academy, which for a time had its own grounds, held its own annual sports meeting. For over a year from the autumn of 1879 it fielded its own rugby team, with Cusack himself as one of its best players. Although a smaller round ball, rather than the conventional oval rugby ball, appears to have been preferred by Cusack's students, his Academy XV was affiliated to the Leinster branch of the Irish Rugby Football Union in November 1880. Then in 1883 the Academy changed to hurling, when its principal was involved in a revival in Dublin of the national game.

2

Since his boyhood Cusack had, according to himself, been interested in athletics.[7] However, before his arrival in the Dublin area in 1874 there is little evidence to support this claim. On the other hand, it has to be remembered that before the 1870s regular reporting of athletics meetings was almost non-existent in Irish provincial newspapers. There is, of course, the episode of Cusack vaulting the gate near Lough Cutra school, and also a reference many years later suggesting some association with athletics in 1872 when he was in Newry.

However, about Cusack's sporting and athletic activities after his appointment to the staff of Blackrock College there is no shortage of information. In addition to participating fully in football and cricket in the school itself, he seems to have joined the Trinity College Rowing Club soon after his arrival in Blackrock. In September 1874, he played in a handball tournament organised by that club. Almost two years later in May 1876, only a month before his wedding, he was still rowing for the TCD club.

In the 1875 Dublin athletics season, Cusack competed in three major sports — the Dublin Amateur Athletic Club's sports in May, the Civil Service Athletic Club's sports in June and the O'Connell Centenary meeting in August. At the first of these he won both the 16 lb and the 42 lb weight events; at the second he won the 16 lb event and came second in the 42 lb event; at the third he was again second in the 42 lb competition. At the May sports he entered as a member of the French College (Blackrock) Cricket Club, and in those of June and August as a member of the DAAC, the sponsor of the June meeting.

Apart from his solitary rowing event in May 1876, Cusack did not again participate in any type of outdoor sport until November 1879, when starting from that month he captained Cusack's Academy XV in the Dublin rugby football competitions. During the three previous years he was, he later explained, fully occupied providing for his family and running his school. By mid-September 1879, as already mentioned, the Cusacks had transferred to the Nelson Street house, and it seems that this move marked an improvement in his position such as to allow a renewed participation by Cusack in athletics. In addition, obesity caused by lack of exercise forced his return to the arena.

Indeed, it was probably some months before his rugby debut in November 1879 that Cusack made a return to the Dublin athletics scene — this time in an administrative capacity. His acceptance of an offer of a seat on the council of the prestigious Irish Champion Athletic Club was the beginning of an important new role for him, that of athletics official.[8] It was one that he was to play for almost four years in three different clubs, and one that was then to lead almost logically to his decision to found the GAA.

Modern field and track athletics in this country began on an organised basis in Trinity College, where the Dublin University Athletic Club was founded in 1857. This was followed in 1867 by the establishment of the Civil Service club. Rural Ireland — particularly Munster, where the traditional events had survived the Famine in wide areas, but to a lesser extent Connacht also — was quick to follow Dublin's lead. Gradually, however, athletics stagnated in Dublin, probably because of the existence of only two permanent clubs, thus confining athletics to a very limited circle of competitors in the city area.

Then the arrival in the early 1870s, more or less together, of two new Dublin clubs, the Dublin Amateur Athletic Club and the Irish Champion Athletic Club, marked a new revival of athletics in the capital. The DAAC seems to have been the first in the field; it held its first annual sports in the summer of 1872. Although it began life in June 1872 as the Royal Irish Athletic Club, the ICAC was regarded by its principal founder, H. W. Dunlop, as really having started in March 1873, the month of its first general meeting.

Although a good deal of rivalry, even some animosity, existed between the DAAC and the ICAC, they were basically different types of clubs. Essentially the DAAC was a conventional athletic club such as would be recognisable today, catering for athletes not eligible for membership of the TCD or Civil Service club. It ran about half-a-dozen meetings in Dublin each season, including one major meeting. Cusack became a member of the DAAC in June 1875, and seems to have remained in it until 1879, when he switched to the ICAC — presumably because of the invitation to a seat on the latter's council.

The ICAC, on the other hand, was from its inception a much more ambitious project. Aiming at a kind of federation of the existing clubs, it was the first of several attempts to impose some form of unified or central control on the management of Irish athletics. Drawing into its membership officers of the various clubs in Dublin and the provinces, the ICAC financed its own expensive trophies and struck its own medals, all of Irish manufacture. It appears to have resented the continued success of the DAAC, which lasted at least to the end of 1878 season. By then the ICAC itself was in deep trouble.

Open to all 'Irish gentlemen amateurs', the ICAC in 1873 inaugurated an annual end-of-season championship meeting in Dublin. At these some or all of the famous four Davin brothers from Carrick-on-Suir competed, and it was almost certainly at one such meeting that Michael Cusack first met the eldest of the Davins, Maurice. Maurice was in fact nominated on several occasions to represent Ireland by the ICAC at international sports meetings in England, where he achieved international fame.

Almost from the start too the ICAC, unlike most other clubs in Dublin, had its own grounds, first at Sydney Parade and from 1874 at Lansdowne Road, now for a century the headquarters of Irish rugby. The controlling body of this game actually grew out of the ICAC, and was the only lasting impact this club made on Irish sporting history. Yet, although the ICAC had only a brief and mostly controversial life, it represented a laudable attempt to introduce into Irish amateur athletics an orderly management system.

Moreover, both the ICAC and the DAAC catered for much more than conventional athletics. Both had sections that also ran (and, in the case of the ICAC, provided facilities for) a whole variety of other activities — cricket, tennis, lacrosse, archery, croquet, even Irish dancing and, significantly in the context of Michael Cusack, rugby football, played occasionally with a round rather than a oval ball. Against this background Cusack's choice in 1879 of rugby as the field game for his pupils is understandable. In any event, there was then no other type of football being played competitively in Dublin.

From its foundation, the ICAC was understandably dominated by officers of the Trinity and Civil Service clubs. Its provincial representatives came from such institutions as the Queen's Colleges of Belfast, Cork and Galway; Armagh Royal School and Portora School, Enniskillen. Its patrons included the Lord Chancellor, five earls, two lords, Queen Victoria's *aide-de-camp* and several other British military top-brass. The ceremonial opening of the grounds at Lansdowne Road in 1874 was performed by the Lord Lieutenant, the Queen's representative in Ireland.

What was the Clare herdsman's son doing in this politically well-heeled company? The answer, it is suggested, is simply that when a serious split, which had developed in the ICAC in 1876, threatened the very existence of the club three years later, Cusack's services were sought by one side or the other — or perhaps by both. Ironically, as will soon appear, he was eventually to preside over the death and burial of the ICAC.

Although he did not take part in any type of sports from May 1876 until the Naas meeting of July 1881, the invitation to take a seat on the ICAC council in 1879 shows that Cusack had continued to watch events from the sideline. Moreover, by then he had also formed, and widely articulated, some radical views on Irish athletics. We can be sure too that long before he published these views in newspaper columns or aired them in any committee rooms 'the Governor', as his pupils affectionately called Cusack, had forcibly expressed them in his own Academy.

3

From the time when he opened his Academy in 1877, if not indeed from his arrival in Blackrock three years earlier, Michael Cusack was regarded in Dublin as something of a character. Like many a self-made man he excluded self-confidence, to a degree that excluded modesty about his achievements and his opinions. Moreover, to an extent that almost amounted to affectation, he never concealed his opinions on politics, sports, religion, literature and education, even — or, one suspects, especially — when he knew that his audience held diametrically opposite views to his. And, although he never visited his native Clare around this time, he naturally sought the company of Claremen in Dublin. One of his earliest friends in the city was Joseph Hynes from the Burren, the owner of the Red Bank Oyster Bar in Dame Street, some of whose employees, Cusack was delighted to discover, were Irish speakers.[9]

It is around this time that we get our first clear picture of Cusack. In appearance he was of just average height, with broad shoulders and powerfully built arms and legs. To the end of his life the writer Oliver Gogarty never forgot Cusack's enormous calves. His plump features and small dark eyes produced a handsome effect, which was heightened by a normally serious facial expression. He sported a thick black bushy beard. By 1880 or so his three-year self-enforced absence from the athletic arena had caused him to put on weight, giving him an impression of portliness, even of obesity.

Understandably, Cusack's mannerisms and even personal habits irked his critics and opponents, who gradually grew in numbers from his arrival in Dublin, and who were not all to be found amongst the city's unionist community. To them he seemed to make a point of emphasising how different he was from the majority of Dubliners. As early as his Blackrock College days his heavy drinking shocked at least one of his teaching colleagues.[10] He dressed in what Dubliners reasonably regarded as homespun rural clothes, often wearing knee-breeches in preference to the conventional trousers, and was usually shod in heavy hob-nailed boots. He frequently carried a stout blackthorn stick, wore a sloppy slouched hat, and spoke in what Dublin folk felt was an unnecessarily loud voice — a feature his own friends noticed to the end of his life.[11]

Yet it would be wrong to regard Cusack as an eccentric; most of his contemporaries did not do so. Within a short time of his arrival in the Dublin area he had become accepted by prominent members of the unionist community, particularly those connected with Trinity College, whose sporting activities he joined and from whose undergraduates he drew many of the pupils in his Academy. Clearly too, his views on athletics must have commended wide respect for him to have been offered a seat on the ICAC council.

Ostensibly, the cause of the split which had developed in the ICAC by the late 1870s was a proposal in 1876 by its founder and dominating figure, H. W. Dunlop, to turn the club into a company so as to finance more expansion at Lansdowne Road. Despite opposition to this scheme all through 1877, Dunlop got it approved in December. However, the opposition continued over the next two years, and in 1878 he commenced litigation in the High Court against his opponents. It was at this stage that Cusack was called in, presumably because of his influence with both camps.

During Cusack's absence from the sports arena in the three years or so from June 1876, evidence had grown suggesting that all was not well with Irish athletics, especially in the Dublin area. As early as October 1877, a plan was published for an Irish National Athletics Committee to control athletics — precisely what the ICAC aimed at too. Although this proposal remained alive for several months, it had died by mid-1878. Before that, however, it had gained wide support from prominent figures in the athletic world, among them Maurice Davin and one Pat Nally from Mayo.

Pat Nally came from a prosperous farming background. Not only was he, all through the 1870s, the most prominent athlete west of the Shannon, he was also a leading figure in the agrarian movement and a top Connacht Fenian. Under his leadership the Fenians in the west had espoused the cause of the small tenant-farmer there, making Nally a bitter opponent of the landlords, who coincidentally were the patrons of athletics too.[12] It is easy to appreciate that he and Cusack had much in common when they met in Dublin, apparently for the only time, in the spring of 1879, before Cusack had joined the ICAC.

P.W. Nally   *Maurice Davin*

Two similar and probably co-ordinated moves, made soon after the meeting of Nally and Cusack, give some idea of their identical views on one aspect of Irish athletics. In September 1879, Nally organised the first National Athletic Sports of Mayo. Held on his father's estate, the patrons of the event were Parnell and the local Home Rule MP — a departure from normal practice that hardly went unnoticed by the Mayo landlords, and an event repeated a year later.[13] Then some six months later, at Easter 1880, Cusack organised a National Athletics Meeting in Dublin, with the objective, he stated, of allowing participation in athletics by the artisan classes.[14] Over a year later again Cusack, with Val Dunbar of the *Irish Sportsman*, was involved in a 'people's sports' held in Dundalk. On 29 June 1881, following a public meeting some weeks earlier protesting against the elitist rules imposed by Dundalk Football Club at its annual sports, 10,000 attended a rival sports meeting, at which Cusack in a speech made the case for a body to control Gaelic sports.[15]

Yet it was clearly not just to the opening of athletics to the man in the street (or on the farm, looked at from Nally's viewpoint) that Cusack and Nally confined their discussion in 1879. Both knew that Irish athletics were then in decline. In the Dublin he had settled in, in 1874, Cusack had found athletics thriving; on his return to sports meetings in 1879, however, he found that all sorts of abuses had crept in, which Nally had criticised in 1877. Professional betting, money prizes, fraudulent handicapping, poor judging, riotous behaviour by exuberant youths, such as had led to the cancellation of the Trinity sports for two years — these were amongst the principal causes of the slump between 1876 and 1879.

Out of this meeting of two men with a common Fenian background, alike in temperament, in love of country and in hatred of injustice, came something more than a mere vague or general consensus on the state of Irish athletics. From the reverence in which Cusack held Nally's memory some twenty years later after his mysterious death in Mountjoy jail, it is clear that it was he who supplied the nationalist motivation that inspired much of Cusack's agitation in Irish athletics in the five years after their 1879 meeting. In 1895, Cusack stated that Nally had in 1879 approved of his scheme to revive Irish games, and in 1899 he stated that nobody had done more than Nally to persuade him to found a body like the GAA.[16] Moreover, evidence that the oral tradition of Nally's impact persisted some twenty-five years after his death is furnished by the otherwise inexplicable inclusion of a photograph of him in O'Sullivan's history of the GAA, although (possibly because the book had to pass the military censor in 1916) there is no reference whatever to Nally in the text.

For Cusack the short-term impact of his meeting with Nally was a decision to try to reform Irish athletics from inside the existing system. Indeed, if one accepts this the question may be asked as to whether he deliberately angled for the invitation from the ICAC, which he apparently joined shortly after the talk with Nally. Acceptance of this invitation gave him his first opportunity to advance his presumably well-known ideas on reform or control of athletics to an audience that, if not very likely at the outset to be sympathetic, might at least be in a position to make new decisions. It was this aim of cleaning up athletics which Cusack was to pursue through three Dublin clubs between 1879 and 1883, until he was finally forced to take what he said was Nally's original advice, and base his campaign on a wholly nationalist foundation.

His position as a leading ICAC member now secure, Cusack seems to have given priority for much of 1880 to ensuring the success of his school's rugby team in Dublin rugby. There are references to games in February, March, April, October, November and December. In September, the club held its annual meeting; at this, when it became clear that the pool of players would be bigger in the new season, it was decided to resume play. Two months later there followed its affiliation to the Irish Rugby Football Union.

Yet, in spite of all this activity on the rugby field, Cusack did not neglect athletics either in 1880. In May at the annual ICAC championship, he was a judge; so was Maurice Davin. During the year a new executive was formed, in a last effort in which Cusack was prominent, to keep alive the ailing ICAC, which had given up its tenancy of Lansdowne Road to Lansdowne rugby club. Then, at a meeting in December of twelve leading members (among them Cusack), it was unanimously decided, in view of the club's accumulated debts, to dissolve the ICAC and to use its property in part-discharge of its liabilities. More significantly, since it indicated his determination to continue to have a voice in the running of athletics, Cusack had in November presided at the foundation of a new club, the City and Suburban Harriers, to specialise in cross-country running.

Rugby once more accounted for a good deal of Cusack's outdoor activities in 1881. Since his Academy team had been disbanded at the end of the 1880 season, he joined the Phoenix football club. There are reports of his participation in its fixtures in January, November and December. One of his team-mates — perhaps the man responsible for his joining the club — was the Tipperary man, Thomas St George McCarthy, Cusack's former pupil, who had come first in an RIC cadetship examination and was to be present in Thurles in 1884 at the foundation of the GAA.

However, as in 1880, Cusack did not in 1881 neglect athletics. In April, he was one of three judges at the championship meeting of a new club, the Cross Country Association of Ireland, of which he was also a prominent member. He chaired a meeting in May called by the CCAI to organise the raising of funds to pay the ICAC's debts, and became treasurer of the new campaign. This move was a failure; the ICAC ended in the Bankruptcy Court and the pioneer Civil Service club official J. T. Hurford was obliged to pay the legal costs.[17] Significantly, Cusack seems to have taken no part in a move to form yet another body, the Amateur Athletics Association of Ireland, which died a lingering death in 1882.

It was in 1881 too that Cusack, now in his thirty-fourth year, had his greatest success as an athlete, one which James Joyce was to immortalise in *Ulysses* over forty years later. Returning to the arena after nearly three years, Cusack first won the 16 lb shot event at the Kildare sports in Naas in July. Later that same month at Lansdowne Road, at the ninth annual championship meeting which had been inaugurated by the now defunct ICAC, he became the Irish 16 lb shot champion, with a throw that was better than the current British standard.

Of greater significance for Irish athletics in the long term was a series of three articles which Cusack, over a six-month period in 1881, contributed to the *Irish Sportsman* at the request of its editor.[18] Although predominantly unionist in outlook, this influential weekly paper had shown intermittent concern for unity in Irish athletics, and it was this theme that Cusack concentrated on. These articles show how his ideas were developing, and explain clearly his dissatisfaction at the existing situation. They also made a moderate and balanced case for a controlling body, in which the inclusion of nationalists was, in Cusack's judgement, essential for it to be genuinely representative of all Irish athletes.

Cusack's first article in April deplored the decline in the genuine athletic spirit, warning that a continuation of this decline would lead to a drop in public morality. Calling for the creation of a public opinion favourable to athletics, he advocated the formation of clubs in every town and college to organise regular local meetings. In mild, even conciliatory, language he pleaded for the restoration of the traditional Irish events in jumping and weight-throwing.

In his second article in July, Cusack made an important and revealing point that goes far to explain, and even to justify, his own deep involvement in athletics from 1879 to 1883. In a country like ours, where political differences were fundamental, sport (he argued) should be a unifying factor, an astonishingly liberal view for one with such strong nationalist views from his youth. However, as one of those 'trying to keep the platform of sport clear of the party spirit', it saddened him that sport suffered in each new political crisis in Ireland.

Here surely is the key to Cusack's whole involvement in the politics of Irish athletics, from the day in 1879 when he took his seat on the ICAC council to the day, probably late in 1883, when he finally severed his connection with what he later bitterly called the West British faction. It was not merely that he believed in the need for a controlling body, nor that he passionately felt that the class-barriers should be broken down, nor even just that nationalists should have a voice in the management of their sports.

What Cusack envisaged, and continued to aim at even after he had founded the GAA in 1884, was a broadly-based sports body that would command the support of the whole Irish sporting community, nationalist and unionist. With this object in mind, he kept what in the light of his later nationalist role in Irish sport may seem now to have been strange company from 1879 to 1883, and also either supported or advocated decisions that seem at variance with his nationalist outlook. Yet, as his 1881 articles show, he never deviated from his belief in the need for Home Rule in Irish athletics. It was clearly so as to be able to advocate this policy (and if possible also to put it into practice) that from 1879 to 1883 he took a hand in the management of one predominantly unionist athletics club after another.

Footnotes

1. *Shamrock,* 1882–1901.
2. See *Sport,* 1.12.1906.
3. *FJ,* 5.6.1885.
4. T. F. O'Sullivan: *Story of the G.A.A.* (Dublin, 1916), p. 3.
5. *Blackrock College Annual,* 1975, p. 20.
6. *Nation,* 28.2.1891.
7. *Nation,* 20.7.1889.
8. *The Gaelic Athlete,* 7.3.1914; *FJ,* 3.8.1896.
9. *CT,* 17.12.1887.
10. *Blackrock College Annual,* 1975, p. 18.
11. *Gaelic Football,* edited by 'Carbery' (Dublin, 1941), article by P. J. Devlin (pp. 163–183); *FJ,* 5.6.1885.
12. See de Búrca, *The GAA: A History* (Dublin, 1980 & 1981), p. 13.
13. de Búrca, pp. 13 & 14.
14. de Búrca, p. 14.
15. *Dundalk Democrat,* June & July 1881; *Irish Daily Independent,* 1.2.1895.
16. *Irish Daily Independent,* 2.2.1895; *United Irishman,* 4.3.1899.
17. *UI,* 14.3.1885.
18. *IS,* 9.4.1881, 2.7.1881, 1.10.1881. For proof of authorship, see *IS,* 10.6.1882 and *Irish Weekly Independent,* Christmas No 1902, p. 29.

Principal Sources

Irish Sportsman, 1872–1884
Shamrock, 1882–1885
Irishman, 1882–1884
Celtic Times, 1887
Irish Champion Athletic Club minute book (custody of Irish Rugby Football Union, Lansdowne Rd., Dublin 4)
Registers of births, Dublin, 1877–1888
James Joyce, *Ulysses* (Penguin Books 1986)
Oliver St J. Gogarty, *Tumbling in the Hay* (Sphere Books, London, 1982)
Thom's Directory, 1876–1901

CHAPTER FOUR

CUSACK GOES FOR HURLING

1882–1883

The year 1882 was a significant one for Michael Cusack. In that year occurred three events which helped to shape the impact he was to make on the Ireland of his time. Yet none of these events in any way broke the consistency of Cusack's advocacy of the cultural aspects of Irish nationalism. On the contrary, everything he did and said in 1882 was a logical extension of what he had been doing and saying since his arrival in Dublin in 1875.

All three events of importance to Cusack in 1882 took place in Dublin in the second half of the year. In two he was personally involved — indeed, dictated the trend of events. Between them, all three were to stimulate him to make decisions that were to have a permanent effect on Irish sport and the Irish language movement in particular, but also in a wider sense on the development of national identity.

The three events concerned led to a quickening of the pace of development, so far as Cusack could influence it, of Irish sport and the language movement. They also produced a more strident expression of his ideas on Irish athletics. In that latter sense 1882 stands out with 1879, the year he took his seat on the ICAC council, and with 1884, the year he was to win Maurice Davin's support for a new sports organisation. In a sense that will shortly become apparent, 1882 was the year that Cusack went Gaelic.

The first of the three events of significance in Cusack's life in 1882 was the rise of the Dublin Athletic Club. The previous year had seen the demise of the two athletic clubs that had dominated the Dublin track for most of the 1870s — the DAAC and the ICAC — and the collapse of the Civil Service club. The new DAC was intended by its founders to replace these three as the city's premier club, and was founded towards the end of April 1882.[1] Its foundation followed several abortive efforts by W. H. Dunlop of the defunct ICAC to start an Irish Amateur Athletics Association — coincidentally (or was it?) the title of the body destined to emerge in 1885 out of unionist opposition to the GAA.

Understandably, in view of his prominent role in the ICAC and his opposition to Dunlop, Cusack was involved in the setting up of the DAC.[2] Just how close was his connection with the starting of the club is not clear. At no time did he become an officer of the DAC, and it was not until 1883 that he joined the club's committee. One suspects that he deliberately kept his distance from those who controlled this new club, almost as if he had little faith in their ability or intention to reform athletics.

However, the DAC was not long in existence before Cusack characteristically tried to influence its affairs. May 1882 had seen the assassinations, in broad daylight in the Phoenix Park in Dublin, of the Chief Secretary at Dublin Castle, Lord Frederick Cavendish, and the Under-Secretary, T. H. Burke, by the extreme Invincible group. The event rocked the nationalist community, and soon the air was thick with both nationalist condemnations and unionist protestations of loyalty. If, as seems unlikely, Cusack had any doubt about which camp most of his DAC colleagues supported, he soon found out.

Suddenly the violent deeds of the shadowy Invincibles intruded on the peaceful discussions of Dublin's newest athletic club, then understandably looking for influential patronage. To the horror of the unionist majority on the DAC committee, a proposal to present a loyal address to the Lord Lieutenant (with a view to making him patron) was countered with a proposal by Cusack. He asked that the Lord Mayor (Charles Dawson, a prominent Home Rule MP), should also be invited to become a patron. In the end nothing came of the idea, for the Lord Lieutenant declined the offer — much to Cusack's delight, presumably.

Having gained a tactical victory in this relatively trivial episode, Cusack now pressed home his advantage by putting forward another and more fundamental idea — not the first time that he did so at an athletic club committee within a five year period. This was a suggestion that open competitions be held, that is, events not confined to so-called gentlemen amateurs. Shrewdly taking advantage of the law-and-order atmosphere generated by the Phoenix Park killings, he pointed out that the amateur rule excluded not only the man in the street but also members of the police, military and naval forces. Their amateur status was breached by 'assisting in the practice of athletic exercises as a means of obtaining a livelihood', to quote from the then current definition of a gentleman amateur.

Almost unbelievably, Cusack won again. The DAC committee agreed to his proposal, specifically accepting an entry for the 16 lb weight event, Cusack's speciality, from a recent former pupil of his, Constable Owen Harte of the RIC. Harte's debut came at the DAC's inaugural meeting in June, when Cusack beat him. But at the annual championship meeting in mid-August (managed for the first time by the DAC) this result was reversed, and Cusack's protegé became the new champion in succession to his former master.[3]

This is how Cusack recalled this episode, in a passage from a letter to an American paper six years later that is typical of his style of invective:

In June 1882 a terrific explosion shook the Irish athletic firmament. The caucus of the Dublin Athletic Club prepared a loyal and touching address for presentation to the Lord Lieutenant ... The address referred with appropriate feeling and touching abhorrence to the 'black deed' of the preceding month, and implored Spencer [the Lord Lieutenant] to bestow his patronage on our most loyal and dutiful club ... I modestly submitted that we might drop the 'address' and by way of manifesting our loyalty permit peelers, soldiers, labourers, tradesmen and artisans to compete at athletic sports. The awkwardness of the situation favoured me, and I came off the victor with a smile ... sweet and ... winning.[4]

To gain two such victories close together — the first purely symbolic, but the second a major break-through in athletic practices — in the tense Irish political atmosphere of 1882 was a real achievement by Cusack, as well as a morale-booster for him. The decision to broaden the category of amateur athlete represented a reward for persistent advocacy of reform, and showed that one at least of his ideas had merit. That he had some support on the DAC committee was established beyond doubt at the club's first annual general meeting in January 1883. Only eight months after the controversial incident of the loyal address, Cusack came second in a ballot for twelve places on the committee.

Yet this experience in 1882 and 1883 of one more (and his last) unionist-dominated athletic club permanently soured Cusack, and was to be decisive in his withholding an invitation to the Orange community of Ulster to join in forming the GAA in 1884. There is evidence that even before the 1883 season opened the honeymoon was over, and that apart from a brief (and again successful) participation in its affairs in 1884, he had parted with what must have been for him the uncongenial company of Courtenay, Hogg, Seddell, Searight, Garner, Faussett and the rest. Significantly, there was no weight event at any of the DAC's three 1883 meetings (at Easter, at Whit and in mid-May); nor is Cusack mentioned in any capacity at any of the three. By then he had abandoned all efforts to unite both sections of Dublin's athletic community, and had moved on to what was literally a new field.

Yet it is surely indicative of Cusack's persuasive personality that some of his former colleagues in the DAC continued to work with him. The names of C. E. Rowland, L. H. Christian, Dick Sproule and J. H. Stewart — all on the DAC committee — will appear again, all to be involved in what was to be for them in every sense a new ball-game. Stewart, a Tyrone man, Cusack had known since 1875; they had been together in both the DAAC and the ICAC. Stewart had supported Cusack's proposal in 1882 for open events, and was to be the only Protestant to achieve vice-presidential office in the early years of the GAA.

2

In mid-August 1882, just three months after Michael Cusack's successes in the DAC, the National Industrial Exhibition — the second event of importance to Cusack in 1882 — opened in Dublin. Such exhibitions had become a regular feature of mid-nineteenth-century Ireland. Belfast had one in 1849, Dublin four between 1853 (when the organiser was that pioneer of Irish railways, William Dargan) and 1872, and Cork in 1872. However, the 1882 exhibition was probably the most successful so far, and because of its origin and scope was to have a lasting effect on Cusack's political philosophy.

In one important respect the 1882 exhibition was unique. It was entirely nationalist-controlled, its organisers refusing all official support or patronage. The event was in fact viewed with hostility by Government circles in Dublin Castle. Towards the end of 1881, following a proposal the previous August by the widely-read Home Rule organ *United Ireland*, a limited company was formed to sponsor the exhibition. Amongst its most active directors were Charles Dawson MP, Lord Mayor of Dublin, Edmund Dwyer Gray

MP, editor of the influential daily *Freeman's Journal*, and other leading nationalist figures in industry.

With enthusiastic encouragement from the entire leadership of the Home Rule movement from Parnell down, the organisers put many months of work into planning the exhibition. A central site was acquired in the Rotunda Gardens at Rutland Square (now the Garden of Remembrance in Parnell Square), where a special modern electrically illuminated glass-and-iron exhibition centre was built. Under Dawson's guidance the Corporation played a prominent part in the elaborate preparations. Amongst the fringe events arranged to coincide with the exhibition's opening were the conferring of the freedom of the city on Parnell and John Dillon, and the holding of a three-day Irish language congress.

When it came to the timing of the exhibition, the organisers showed a combination of daring and ingenuity that amounted to a brilliant victory over the Government. To achieve the maximum public impact the opening was fixed to coincide with the unveiling on 15 August of the O'Connell Monument in Sackville (now O'Connell) Street. An enormous industrial parade through Dublin would precede the formal opening ceremony in the Rotunda Gardens. In this way the tens of thousands of visitors from the provinces expected in Dublin would witness two major events with a strong Home Rule bias.

So elaborate were the preparations that the authorities — not for the first time since the Fenian scare of the 1860s — suspected that a rebellion was being planned. Indeed, an RIC circular that fell into nationalist hands actually warned of the danger of 'Fenian suspects' supporting the Dublin events. Yet, for fear of provoking such an outbreak, the massive police reinforcements brought in for the day were kept discreetly out of sight, the central city area being taken over by volunteer stewards. In the event the parade, the unveiling of the statue and the opening of the exhibition all passed off quietly, the crowds proving to be exceptionally good humoured and disciplined.

Far surpassing the formalities at the O'Connell monument itself, the hour-long procession was one of the most colourful spectacles Dublin had seen for decades, with floats and carriages mounted by all the ancient city trade guilds dominating. Significantly, it was watched by crowds far bigger than had attended the O'Connell Centenary demonstration in 1875. Starting from the Mansion House, the parade took a circuitous route that brought it past the most historic parts of old Dublin. If, as seems certain, Cusack, with his family, was one of the tens of thousands of spectators lining the streets, a prominent bakery exhibit with an inscription in Irish could not have escaped his attention.

The National Industrial Exhibition itself displayed an almost incredible variety of Irish products — industrial, agricultural and artistic. Clothing, machinery (including an entire railway train), food, drink, minerals, displayed by employers, tradesmen, guilds and unions — all were represented in what amounted to an astonishing demonstration of Irish enterprise, which centuries of official discriminatory policy by Britain had failed to kill. Little wonder that for weeks after crowds packed the Rotunda Gardens, many coming from distant parts of the island.

This great demonstration of Irish industry made a deep and lasting impact on Michael Cusack. This became clear from his extensive coverage of native trades when five years later he was editing his own newspaper, the weekly *Celtic Times*. Not only did he put the encouragement of native industry first among the four aims of the paper. He also filled many columns every week reporting the proceedings of trade guilds and trade unions, boosting the achievements of successful industries and investigating the potentialities of newer industrial ventures.

Even in 1882 and 1883, however, it was evident that Cusack had been deeply impressed by the range of exhibits in the Rotunda. In June 1882 he began a thirty-year association with the weekly magazine *The Shamrock*, beginning an educational feature for boys and soon adding an educational feature for post-primary education. Cusack's writings in this widely-read periodical — the principal source of knowledge about his views on many topics — contain several laudatory references in 1882 and 1883 to the success of the industrial exhibition, and to the need to support Irish industry in preference to foreign goods. This was a theme he expanded on in his *Celtic Times* in 1887, and was still speaking on in public almost to his death nearly twenty years later.

It was around this time too that Cusack became an ardent advocate of the ideas put forward in the *Nation* of the 1840s by the Young Ireland leader and thinker, Thomas Davis. From several references from 1882 onwards it is evident that Cusack had immersed himself in Davis's writings. He believed that to read Davis made one a more confirmed nationalist, and he quoted and borrowed freely from Davis and urged his *Shamrock* readers to study Davis. Contrariwise, he gave no evidence that he had any comparable admiration for O'Connell, despite all the praise heaped on the Liberator in 1882 by the Home Rule leaders.

3

Whatever doubts one may have about Cusack having watched the industrial parade passing through central Dublin on 15 August 1882, one has none at all about his attendance at the Irish Language Congress which opened later that same day in the offices of the Society for the Preservation of the Irish Language at 19 Kildare Street. As was customary for such bodies, the SPIL, which organised the congress, published a verbatim report of the proceedings of the three-day event, and Michael Cusack was among the attendance of over sixty.

Curiously, for one who for the rest of his life was to champion the cause of the Irish language, it was only some eight months earlier that Cusack had first publicly associated himself with the language movement. Moreover, although he was later to link the revival of Irish with other aspects of Irish culture, he had not yet developed (and certainly not articulated) any such idea by 1882. Indeed, the circumstances surrounding this new and sudden interest in the language of Cusack's boyhood in Clare thirty years earlier force one to wonder if it would ever have been kindled but for his dissatisfaction with the relative lethargy of those then promoting the revival of Irish.

Founded back in 1876 not long after Cusack's arrival in the Dublin area, the SPIL did much useful work for the Irish language in its early years — pleading the cause of the people of the Irish-speaking districts, publishing grammars and textbooks, lobbying prominent Home Rule figures, getting Irish recognised as a school subject and persuading the educational authorities to pay fees to teachers for teaching Irish. However, in 1879 there was a split, when the two original members of the Society, Fr John Nolan ODC and David Comyn, broke away to found the Gaelic Union for the Preservation and Cultivation of the Irish Language.

Precisely what the cause of this dissension was is not clear; but it all seems to have been done in a gentlemanly way. Both bodies continued to use the same premises, to have the same patron (Archbishop Croke of Cashel) and to have tolerated dual membership. Perhaps, indeed, for some in the Gaelic Union there was too much friendliness, for in January 1882 there was some kind of *coup* or purge. Formalised by a change or upgrading of the Gaelic Union from a committee to an independent society, this was important enough for those who took part in it or supported it to regard that event as marking the foundation of a new Gaelic Union.

At this stage Michael Cusack takes the stage. Although it is unlikely that he had even been in the SPIL, he was clearly well informed of its doings and he did not think a lot of them. Also, in spirit at least he approved of the 1879 breakaway that had led to the GU; at any rate he certainly supported the motives of those responsible for the secession. If, as seems possible, he was a committee member of the GU from 1881, he may even have been one of those behind the 1882 purge, for from then on he became first very active and soon very prominent in the activities of the GU.

Although he was certainly an officer of the GU by 1882, it seems that it was in a personal capacity as a friend of the Irish language, rather than as a GU delegate, that Cusack attended the SPIL's Irish language congress in August 1882. How undeveloped his ideas on Irish culture generally still were is evident from an uncharacteristic (not to say eccentric) intervention he made on the second day, 16 August, during a discussion of a a formal talk given by R. J. O'Duffy, the Secretary of the SPIL.

O'Duffy had concluded with an emotional appeal for public support for the Irish language. They should get public opinion behind them; the country's honour was at stake; if they lost that proud distinguishing mark of a nation, a living language, they would have lost one of the grandest memorials of the race. Astonishingly, Cusack criticised this line as being injudicious; it would, he argued, be interpreted as political in tone, whereas the SPIL belonged to no party and was politically neutral.

Perhaps Cusack's criticism was merely a reflection of his dislike of the SPIL, which in his view had put too little emphasis on the speaking of the language. On the other hand, he may have felt that O'Duffy's mild nationalist approach might offend the many anti- or non-nationalists then supporting the SPIL and the GU. One cannot help feeling that if he had similarly toned down his own strong nationalist views in the various athletic bodies he had been involved in over the previous five years, it is little wonder that he got nowhere with his campaign for Home Rule in Irish athletics.

For almost five years from the start of the 'new' Gaelic Union

— from January 1882 to December 1886 — Cusack was an active, indeed possibly the most active, committee member of the Union. The committee frequently met in his Academy. As a result of pressure from him it began at last to keep proper minutes. At his suggestion it commenced in February 1882 to hold Irish classes — in a room he provided in his Academy and under arrangements drawn up (one might almost say dictated) by him.

Nor was this by any means the whole of Cusack's involvement in the running of the Gaelic Union. When in August 1882 it needed a treasurer he took on the job, holding it for some three years. When two months later the committee felt that a special effort to raise funds for its projected journal was needed, Cusack also willingly, indeed enthusiastically, undertook this substantial extra chore. When in 1883 Archbishop Croke urged a healing of the breach with the SPIL, Cusack was one of the GU delegates to the abortive talks.

One of the probable reasons for the 1879 split in the SPIL was the slowness, or perhaps downright refusal, of the Society to start its own journal or organ. Predictably, the GU got around to considering a similar idea some months after its re-formation in 1882. From the moment in October when a decision to publish was taken, the projected journal had no more energetic supporter than the treasurer, Cusack, who seems to have taken the lead in all the details that led to the actual launching in November of the *Gaelic Journal*.

To suggest that the journal was an instant success would be misleading. Hurriedly planned on a shaky financial base by a group of amateurs at a time when the nationalist press could find no demand for items in the Irish language, it was in trouble from the start. Editorial incompetency, excessive print runs and shortage of money, all experienced in the paper's first few years, were interconnected problems. However, there is no evidence to connect Cusack in a major sense with any of these blunders.

Yet, astonishingly, the journal survived for well over a quarter of a century, and a century later is accepted to have been a landmark in modern publications in the Irish language. One of its editors was Eoin MacNeill, the principal founder of the Gaelic League in 1893. No less distinguished a figure in the language revival movement than Douglas Hyde later referred to the journal as the start of the resurrection of modern Irish.

Although Cusack had parted company with the committee of the Gaelic Union by 1887, it left an impact on him. The similarity between its title and the earliest title of the GAA is obvious, and the selection of Archbishop Croke as the GAA's first patron was no coincidence. Just why Cusack left the GU is not clear; but one does not have to look far to find a reason. By late 1886 he was about to launch his own publication on a weekly basis. Moreover, long before then he had found another aspect of Irish culture to champion, which had pushed into second place in his priorities his interest in the language movement.

4

The revival of hurling began on the second last day of 1882 at an informal meeting held in the College of Surgeons in Dublin. In the lecture-room of Dr Hugh Alexander Auchinleck, a lecturer in the Carmichael School of Medicine, a small group of men met 'for the purpose of taking steps to re-establish the national game of hurling.' A provisional committee of eight — Auchinleck, Michael Cusack, W. Burke, F. F. Bodkin, H. Cooke, L. H. Christian, W. Bell and J. S. Evans, with F. A. Potterton as its secretary — was appointed to draw up rules for the proposed Dublin Hurling Club.

Five days later the same group with some others, in particular C. E. Rowland of the Phoenix Hurley Club, met again. The DHC was formally established, a set of rules adopted and officers elected. Auchinleck was the unanimous choice as president; Cusack became vice-president, and Christian honorary secretary and treasurer. A new ten-man committee consisted of Bell, Bodkin, Burke and Cooke of the provisional committee, with the three Potterton brothers (F.A., R.M. and W.), the two Rowlands (C.E. and E.P.) and L. Hamilton. The opening game or practice session of the new club was fixed for 13 January in the Nine Acres of the Phoenix Park, and the first committee meeting for 8 January in Cusack's Academy.

The meeting on 8 January learned that, although the All-Ireland Polo Club had agreed to the use of its pitch by the DHC, the session fixed for 13 January could not be held, for two reasons. The first was that the date clashed with a harriers meeting at Dollymount in which DHC members were involved. More serious was the discovery by those charged with obtaining hurleys and balls that nobody in Dublin knew how to make them because hurling had for long been extinct in the city.

It was not until early February that enough hurleys were available to hold the first practice on 3 February. Then and at the second session a week later those attending picked two teams; Cusack was among the players on both occasions, captaining the winning side on 10 February. A third session, held two weeks later on 24 February, when with the permission of the Board of Works the DHC used the former Phoenix Rugby Club's pavilion, proved to be the last DHC outing. By then the club had collapsed.

Behind these strange facts lies the strange story of this first attempt to revive hurling, a venture that seemingly ended in unexplained failure. Yet almost incredibly, through Cusack's growing obsession with hurling over the next year or more, this failure was to lead to the game's preservation from extinction and to its ultimate countrywide revival through the foundation by Cusack, eighteen months later, of the GAA.

That the full story of the short-lived, and at times mysterious, episode of the DHC is now unlikely ever to be fully known has to be conceded. So has the fact that some of the known information about the club is capable of conflicting interpretations. Not the least important of the unanswered (and now probably unanswerable) questions about the DHC is why Cusack, who was intimately associated with the club from the start, never publicly explained its failure.

Crucial to the rise of the DHC was the existence in Dublin for some years before 1882 of a game called hurley, somewhat akin to modern field hockey, which seems to have gone into a decline around the time of the foundation of the DHC.[5] One interpretation of the available information is that the DHC was an attempt to fill the gap caused by the expected demise of hurley. Alternatively, if (as can undoubtedly be argued) hurley was about to spread again, the DHC was a deliberate attempt to replace hurley by what was pointedly called hurling.

Whichever of the two explanations for the rise of the DHC is the correct one, it seems probable that among the club's founders were some at least who had no use for hurley (or for those in charge of it), or who felt that hurley was only a debased form of the traditional game of hurling. One can easily understand that following his experiences with the ICAC and the DAC, and (not least) his understandable elation over his success with the *Gaelic Journal,* Cusack would have sided with this group. To such people the possibility that hurley was not a debased form of hurling would be irrelevant; what would count with them would be their (perhaps prejudiced) belief to the contrary.

Similarly, whether or not Cusack was the prime mover in the foundation of the DHC is also irrelevant, for he certainly took a prominent part in it from the early meetings, but not (significantly) for the whole of its short life. Given his known views on hurling from early 1883 onwards, one can have little doubt that references like 'the national game', 'the superiority of the latter game' (hurling) and 'the national movement', all to be found as early as the reports of the preliminary meeting, were almost certainly inspired by Cusack. His election as vice-president and his attendance at at least five of the ten meetings held clearly indicate his leading role in the club's early affairs.

A glance through the twelve simple playing-rules of the DHC (one of which contains only twelve words) strongly suggests that Cusack had a major input in their drafting.[6] While in some respects containing features one associates with hockey, in others they anticipate the rules of the game controlled by the GAA from November 1884. On the whole they seem to owe little to the rival game they were intended to displace, as if Cusack and his fellow committee-members wished to distance themselves widely from hurley.

The playing pitch was 150 yards long. Pushing, holding and tripping were forbidden; but solo runs such as would be recognised a century later were expressly allowed. On the other hand, scores (goals) could only be obtained by driving the ball below the cross-bar, and the ball could not be touched with either hand or foot. 'Crooking of hurls' was prohibited, but the ball could be caught in the hand and 'tossed vertically' to be struck.

Another major difference between hurley and hurling was in the type of hurl. The stick used by the Trinity College hurley players appears to have been as slender as the modern hockey stick; the DHC chose a heavy, wide *camán*. Two patterns were sent by Cusack to Fitzsimons's factory for the DHC, twenty-two being ordered. Fitzsimons, however, made forty-two, which cost two shillings (10p) each and one ball for four shillings (20p). Since a substantial surplus was left when the club collapsed, it is likely that Cusack kept these unused sticks for his next (and more successful) revival of hurling in the autumn of 1883.

With Cusack, the leading figures in the DHC seem to have been Hugh Auchinleck, Lloyd Christian and Frank Potterton. 'Bones' Christian, as he was known to his rivals on the athletic track, had been a friend of Cusack since 1875. Potterton, a colleague of Cusack

DUBLIN HURLING CLUB.

A largely attended general meeting of this club was held lately at 85 York-street to adopt a constitution and amend the rules of the game, Dr. H. Auchinleck, F.R.C.S.I., in the chair. After some discussion, the following rules for playing the game were adopted :—

1. The goal posts shall be pitched 150 yards apart, and each goal shall be formed by two upright posts, eight feet in height, crossed by a horizontal bar, and the posts shall be ten foot apart.

2. That a goal shall be obtained by the ball being driven beneath the [horizontal bar and between the posts.

3. That the ball shall not be struck or propelled in any way by anything save the hurl.

4. The ball, when raised by means of the hurl alone, may be caught in the hand and tossed vertically for the purpose of being struck by the hurl.

5. The ball may be carried (when raised as in 4) any distance by means of the hurl, or tossed forward, and again caught by the same instrument.

6. That the goal line be a continuation of the actual line between the posts to a distance of 50 yards on each side.

7. That when a ball is driven behind this line it shall be considered dead until driven into the field of play by the goal-keeper or any player he may appoint standing in the immediate front of the goal.

8. That in the melee (i.e., when more than one player is in direct play with the ball) no player shall swing his hurl, or strike with back of same, save when the ball is in the air.

9. That no crooking or clashing of hurls be admitted, and that the hurls be employed solely to guard the person of the player, and to stop, strike, or carry the ball.

10. Should the ball cross the boundary of touch it shall be tossed out at right angles with the touch line into the field of play by a player on the opposite side to the player that last struck it previous to going into touch.

11. A player is not allowed to push, hold, or trip an adversary.

12. That in the event of infringements of Rules 3, 8, 9, or 11, the ball be brought back on appeal to the umpire to where the infringement occurred and a bully formed there.

Rules of Dublin Hurling Club, 1883. From Irish Sportsman

on the teaching staff of Kilkenny College in 1876, was the son of the proprietor of a private school flourishing in Newry when Cusack was there. Auchinleck, a Tyrone man two years younger than Cusack, had been educated at Potterton's Academy in Newry, was later a professor in the College of Surgeons and may have seen hurling or shinty (or both) played in his boyhood in the Donegal or Tyrone countryside near his native Strabane.

All through the DHC's short life its members displayed an ambivalent attitude to the game they were trying to replace. Up to a point they tried to be conciliatory. The club should not, they decided unanimously, be 'antagonistic' to any existing sports; hence the cancellation (already mentioned) of the opening practice. An anonymous DHC committee-man publicly denied that his club wished to cause ill-feeling among hurley-men against hurling; the club, he insisted, 'was anxious to secure their co-operation...' Moreover, several DHC men (including some of the committee) continued to play hurley — among them Dick Sproule (formerly of the DAC), Rowland, Christian and Bell.

On the other hand, one cannot avoid the impression that the feeling of many in the DHC was one of hostility, and even aggression, towards hurley. From the start there was an undisguised attempt to poach players from the rival game. Repeated public invitations were made to 'members of recognised clubs' (clearly meaning hurley clubs) to join the DHC sessions, and offers of free hurls were made.

In this attacking policy towards hurley one suspects that, although he was not alone in his attitude, Cusack played a leading role. He was almost certainly the 'ancient Irish hurler' who apparently abused hurley men at one of the games. They were quick to reply in kind (but in print only) by claiming that only 'beardless youths' played their games, an obvious reference to Cusack, then sporting a thick bushy black beard.

To be fair to the DHC, most of the unpleasantness between the two codes was begun by the hurley men. They found influential support among the sporting journalists, who showed obvious prejudice in their criticism of hurling, and who also ignored a request by the DHC that they distinguish clearly between hurley and hurling. A DHC allegation that the hurley clubs tried to smother hurling at birth went unanswered; so did a claim that the DHC had 'to struggle against insuperable obstacles'. Coupled with this latter allegation was a plea (which the press ignored) to give hurling a chance to develop before comparing it unfavourably with the longer-established hurley.

Despite what looks suspiciously like an attempt to cover up by the sparsest of minutes, the DHC records show signs of dissension as the early weeks of 1883 passed. What the cause was is difficult to state; but the facts, bare though they are, speak for themselves. After three seemingly harmonious committee meetings in January, E.P. Rowland, a prominent hurley player, resigned at the fourth. There followed three February meetings from which Cusack was missing, none in March, and one in mid-April which unanimously decided to stop playing 'for the present'. Six months later, in October, an unrecorded general meeting appears to have wound up the DHC.

With the assistance of contemporary press reports, nearly all unsympathetic, one can clearly ascertain one cause of the collapse, while from the minutes one can guess at another. From the start, despite an initial display of public interest, the DHC failed to attract more than a handful of players; 'very indifferent support' Cusack called it six years later.[7] In published reports that were clearly supplied by Christian the attendances at the first and second sessions were called respectively 'smallish' and comprising 'twenty players'. Presumably the initial delay in persuading Fitzsimons's timber factory on the south quays to make hurls and balls did not help; neither did the unusually cold wet weather of February 1883.

Little wonder that by late January the hurley commentators were boasting that, although their game's detractors wished it to collapse, it was showing no signs of surrender. That same week the widely-respected Rowland of Phoenix Hurley Club left the DHC; if he had been one of the deputation from an influential hurley club that was taken as 'an omen of success' on 30 December, his departure was equally ominous.

The less obvious cause of dissention was the committee's reaction to spectators. From the first session, doubtless attracted by the advance publicity, the public came to watch. In line with the initial invitation 'to join in the national movement', some spectators, who were almost certainly hurling players or supporters from outside Dublin living in the city, did so — presumably using the spare hurleys. However, this fraternisation was abruptly ended by a decision of the committee on 22 February (taken in Cusack's absence) to confine future matches to 'members, intending members and members of recognised clubs'. In view of the vital role he assigned to spectators later that same year at the same venue, it can safely be assumed that Cusack was against the 22 February decision. Indeed, his opposition may explain the six-week period that elapsed before the meeting on 21 April, which resolved to have no more matches 'for the present'.

If, as suggested, the DHC committee divided on the question of admission of outsiders who were non-hurley men, Cusack's almost total silence subsequently on the club's collapse — 'a ludicrous attempt' he called it in 1889[8] — is understandable. If he regarded hurley as not the genuine article — he once called it 'a beggerly thing' — he would hardly have regarded the Trinity clique which controlled it as representative of the average Irishman. Indeed, his 1881 warning in the *Irish Sportsman*, that what the rugby men of the ICAC needed was 'a strip of green across their colours and their ground', was equally apt in 1883.

Some biographical details of a few of the DHC members suggest that the ordinary Irishman of probable nationalist or Catholic background was decidedly in the minority. James Nolan was in the Arrears Office of the Land Commission, and Hugh Cooke was a court official. William Burke was a Board of Works employee in the Phoenix Park, and William J. O'Connor worked in Pim's drapery store in South Great George's Street.

From somewhat different backgrounds from those four came some of the more prominent members of the club. Lloyd Christian, E.S. Donne and William Bell were officials of the Royal Bank, while Robert Potterton had a doctorate in laws from Trinity College. As already mentioned, his brother Frank was a teacher, while Dr Auchinleck was a medical lecturer, having become a Fellow of the Royal College of Surgeons in Ireland in 1881.

That a group of mostly middle-class urban Protestants, presumably of unionist persuasion, should in the Ireland of 1882-83, against the background of Parnell's growing power and the Invincible killings, have come together to foster the national game of hurling, in opposition to the existing version controlled from Trinity College, was surprising. Even more remarkable was the fact that they envisaged not just one club, but in time an association of clubs. This is clear not merely from the use of the phrase 'national movement', but also from the minute-books. Meticulously kept by Christian, they show that a life of at least four years was optimistically planned for the DHC.

Yet, inexplicably, for nearly all those involved in the DHC this was a once-only effort to revive hurling. The sole known exception was, of course, Michael Cusack, who only a few short months later, after the failure of the DHC, made yet another effort — this time almost single-handed, but this time too with much greater success.

Footnotes
1. *Irish Weekly Independent,* Christmas No 1902, p. 29; *FJ,* 3.8.1896.
2. *Gaelic Athlete,* 7.3.1914; *Shan Van Vocht,* Vol. 2 (1897), p. 147.
3. *FJ,* 31.10.1885; *IS,* 19.7.1884.
4. *Chicago Citizen,* 22.9.1888.
5. Dublin University Athletic Council, minutes, 22.5.1883 (TCD, MS 2257).
6. See *IS,* 24.2.1883, for amended version.
7. *Nation,* 6.7.1889.
8. *Nation,* 6.7.1889.

Principal Sources

Celtic Times, 1887

Daily Express, 1883 (Jan.-Mar.)

FJ, 1882 (Aug.-Dec.) and 1883 (Jan. and Feb.)

Irish Sportsmen, 1882 and 1883

Irish Times, 1883 (Jan. and Feb.)

Nation, 1882 (Aug.-Dec.)

Shamrock, 1882 (June-Dec.); 1883 and 1884

Sport, 1883

United Ireland, 1885

Annual Register, 1882

Dublin Hurling Club minutes (custody of Miss P. O'Connell, UCG; copy loaned by Edmund Van Esbeck)

Gaelic Journal, 1882

Gaelic Union minutes 1882-1886

SPIL reports 1878-1889 and Irish Language Congress report 1882

H. Hartnell, *Guide to National Industrial Exhibition* (Dublin, 1882)

Reámhchonraitheoirí, M. Ní Mhuiríosa (Dublin, 1968)

CHAPTER FIVE

THE PATH TO HAYES'S HOTEL

1883–1884

What made Michael Cusack decide to revive hurling? Sooner or later an attempt must be made to answer this single most important question about the foundation of the GAA. For, but for the inclusion in Cusack's programme for the reform of Irish athletics of both hurling and what came to be called Gaelic Football, the GAA as we know it today would not exist. Moreover, all the evidence strongly points to the conclusion that hurling was only added by Cusack as late as December 1882, and football by Davin as late as October 1884.

Considering the impact in both the cultural and the political contexts which the GAA made on Irish society in its first forty years, it is perhaps worth reflecting momentarily on the type of sports body that Cusack would have founded but for his late conversion to hurling and Davin's partiality for football. Instead of the association we now know that emerged from the Thurles meeting of November 1884, what Cusack would have founded — and would have been content to the end of 1882 to have founded — would have been a body catering solely for athletics.

By a curious coincidence, forty years after Cusack's conversion to hurling just such a body was founded with the establishment (largely on the initiative of prominent GAA personalities) in 1922 of the National Athletic and Cycling Association (NACA). With the then recent creation of a separate Irish state, the need for a body like the NACA had become essential to allow Irish athletes to compete as such for the first time in the modern Olympic Games. For most of the preceding forty years (from 1885 to 1922), because of the predominantly nationalist complexion of the GAA, a rival body, the IAAA, had catered for athletes who either stayed or were kept outside the GAA.

Before giving an account of Cusack's second, and successful, hurling revival it is necessary to try to grapple with the problem of what made him decide to launch such a revival at all. For a start, it has to be admitted that the available evidence prevents the question from being answered with anything like certainty. To make matters worse, the possibility of further facts coming to light now so long after Cusack's death seems remote. As a result, mainly because of insufficient reliable information, this central problem of Cusack's motivation must remain something of a mystery. For this unsatisfactory state of affairs Cusack himself is largely to blame, because his later statements — scattered, biassed, inadequate, even contradictory — about the events of 1882-1884 do nothing to help solve this fundamental mystery.

The most that can be done is to marshal what appear to be the salient relevant facts, and then suggest an answer. At the same time, the possibility has to be frankly conceded that some at least of those facts admit of one or more quite different answers.

So far as is known, Cusack never publicly showed any interest in hurling before he participated in the foundation of the Dublin Hurling Club at the end of 1882. For this reason it is tempting, indeed natural, to concentrate on that year in searching for his motivation. As the previous chapter has shown, 1882 was certainly a significant year for Cusack. After his triumphs with the Dublin Athletic Club and the *Gaelic Journal* he may have been encouraged to believe that he could achieve more successes — such as a revival of hurling, if by any chance he had been privately brooding on such a project.

One theory, based wholly on 1882, but (it will be suggested) on only one aspect of Cusack's activities that year, has already been hinted at — and advanced elsewhere too. It runs simply like this: In the immediate aftermath of his success in launching the *Gaelic Journal* — to be precise, as a direct result of the feeling of euphoria which that event understandably caused him — Cusack spontaneously decided to try for a similar success in another neglected sphere of Irish culture.

This, however, appears to be too restricted an explanation of Cusack's apparently sudden conversion in 1882 to the need to revive hurling. In particular, without even going beyond that year it takes no account of two other events (mentioned in the previous chapter) which seem to have made an impact on him — his own success in persuading the Dublin Athletic Club to broaden the category of amateur athlete and the triumph of the Home Rule movement (of which he was now a staunch supporter) with the National Industrial Exhibition.

In one sense, admittedly, when one takes into account the DAC episode and the industrial exhibition one is reinforcing the 'spontaneous theory'. Indeed, a comment by Cusack himself in 1883, to the effect that the nation was going through a period of revivals, seems to give more force to this argument. Moreover, supporters of this theory can point to the fact that this revealing remark occurred in an article which specifically mentioned the hurling revival recently launched by the Dublin Hurling Club.

On the other hand, an important point about Cusack's public career up to 1882 is surely missed if one concentrates solely on one year to find out why he decided to take such a prominent part in the DHC — even though that year was the one in which his interest in reviving hurling was apparently awakened. From the time in 1879 when he took his seat on the ICAC Council — probably even earlier, since that event was presumably preceded by a period of perhaps several years, publicly airing his views on Irish athletics — there was a thread of consistency running through all Cusack's various involvements in the management of athletics. This persistent theme can be stated in four words — Home Rule for athletics.

Indeed, Home Rule in the wider and more commonly used sense is the basis of another theory which seeks to explain why Cusack decided to revive hurling. Stated simply, it goes like this. Not only was he a political nationalist but a cultural one too, one of a rare breed in the 1880s. As such he felt it to be his mission to advance Irish culture, specifically to fill out the national identity to which, he hoped, Home Rule in politics would give recognition. For years he had worked for Home Rule in athletics; recently he had struck a blow for the Irish language; now he would try to do the same for the national ball-game.

However, this superficially attractive idea is inapplicable to the Cusack of 1882 or earlier. That it is reasonably accurate when applied to a later Cusack is undeniable; but it simply does not fit the Cusack we know almost to the end of 1882. Until at least 1883, and probably for several years afterwards, the only Home Rule he was interested in was Home Rule for athletics. There is no indication that he had yet given any thought to a wider concept of self-government — except, of course, to support the Home Rule movement as a private citizen.

If Michael Cusack was indeed by 1882 a supporter of what a later generation called the Sinn Féin philosophy, he succeeded in concealing this fact until some time after he founded the GAA in 1884. That he was an orthodox constitutional nationalist is not in doubt, after having (as already suggested) briefly flirted with physical force in his late teens. Yet between the typical moderate Home Ruler of the 1880s and the full-blooded supporter of cultural nationalism, like the average member of Sinn Féin in the early 1900s, there was a big difference both in practice and in theory.

Whatever about his later political philosophy (of which more in a subsequent chapter) Cusack's nationalism before 1883 appears to have been of the simplest brand. That he passionately desired Irishmen to gain control of their athletic pursuits is abundantly clear; but so did many others then involved in Irish athletics who politically were unionists to the core. That he sincerely wanted to see Irish restored as a vernacular tongue is equally undeniable; but neither is the fact that, as his 1882 speech at the Irish Language Congress showed, he was then prepared to trim his political sails to help Irish regain the position of prominence it had lost since the Famine period.

It is true that Cusack's political outlook broadened fairly rapidly in the mid-1880s. But, to appreciate just where hurling stood in his scale of priorities even as late as the autumn of 1884, one has only to observe the way in which he tagged on its revival as a kind of minor appendage to the body he was planning for the reform and democratisation of Irish athletics. One cannot in this context ignore the fact that, when ultimately he came to settle on a name for this body, hurling found no place in the title of the Gaelic Athletic Association — nor, indeed, in either of the two earlier titles he is known to have considered for the GAA.

In these circumstances, perhaps a brief attempt to analyse what Home Rule for Irish athletics meant to Cusack may not be out of place. For that, after all, was his main aim for Irish sport for at least the ten years starting in 1874. It meant principally, of course, that athletics (not, it should be noted, hurling, at least before the foundation of the DHC at the end of 1882) in this country should be controlled by Irishmen. These Irishmen should, in Cusack's view, not be confined to a particular section of the community but should be representative of the population in general, both nationalist and unionist.

It meant too that priority should be given by Irish athletes to the traditional events (such as weights and jumps) in which our people had always excelled, or at least specialised. It meant further that sports meetings should be open to all classes and creeds, rather than confined to the better-off sections of the urban community, as was still the position in Dublin in 1884, despite all Cusack's efforts over the previous decade.

Much of this may seem to have little connection with a sudden passion on Cusack's part to revive hurling. Yet what is significant, it is suggested, is the timing of his first public display of interest in that game. This came only months after his two victories over the DAC committee, when (as already recorded) he frustrated its attempt to make the Lord Lieutenant a patron of the club and succeeded in persuading the committee to run an open meeting. Despite these successes, however, it is clear that the hostility he then experienced finished him permanently with unionist-dominated athletic clubs.

When, only a few short months after the end of the 1882 athletics season, the formation of a club to revive hurling was mooted, Cusack must have seen in such a venture a heaven-sent opportunity to show those running athletics (of whom, to him, the DAC committee members were typical) what he thought of them. For if hurling was to be revived, it could only be at the expense of hurley; and those who controlled hurley were to a large extent those who controlled athletics. So, if hurling displaced hurley, it would be a major defeat for Cusack's opponents — that is, for those who had consistently blocked his ideas for reform of athletics for years.

Although he himself never publicly admitted as much, it is impossible to avoid the conclusion that the continued existence of hurley in the Dublin area since his arrival there in 1874 was a factor in Cusack's decision to support the DHC's move to revive hurling. Admittedly it is difficult — though not impossible — to ascertain his views on hurley; but his non-participation in the game tells its own story. Hurley, its promoters claimed, was the authentic national game of the Irish. For over a decade it was promoted from Trinity College. During most of that same decade Cusack maintained a wide circle of acquaintances in Trinity, participating with its sportsmen in rowing, cricket, football and athletics. Yet he never took the slightest interest in hurley.

When only months after his frustrating experience with the DAC the DHC was proposed, it must have seemed to Cusack to be an ideal chance to wrest control of the national game from those who for so long (and, in his view, on purely political grounds) had opposed his ideas to reform atheltics. It was, after all, the same 'foreign faction' (his normal and contemptuous term for the dominant unionist clique in Dublin athletics) that managed both athletics and hurley. Even a random glance at reports of both these sporting activities shows the extent to which leading hurley-men were involved in athletics, and vice versa.

How and why, after the collapse of the DHC — with the inevitable return of most of its leading members to athletics or hurley or both — Cusack first extended his campaign for reform of athletics outside Dublin, then linked it with a new drive to revive hurling, and finally made the revival of hurling a twin aim with the reform of athletics, remains to be told next.

2

As soon as it became clear to him that the Dublin Hurling Club would not survive the spring of 1883, Michael Cusack launched a remarkable one-man campaign that was to culminate twenty months later in the foundation of the GAA. For most of this period all the prominent personalities, bodies and organs involved in Irish sport were against him. Not until the autumn of 1884 was he to make a breakthrough; only then did he win the support which he correctly judged to be sufficiently influential to justify the launch of his new sports body that winter.

The first weapon Cusack used to launch this new campaign early in 1883 showed a deliberate and important change of emphasis — from town to country. By now the weekly educational column he had been conducting in the *Shamrock* magazine since the previous summer had built up a wide readership, a high proportion of which, because of the nature of the feature, came from outside Dublin. It was to this section of the community that he now appealed for support in the revival of hurling, while continuing his campaign to reform athletics largely through personal contacts.

The timing of Cusack's references to hurling in the *Shamrock* in 1883 shows that from quite an early stage in the life of the DHC he was pessimistic about the club's future. It cannot have been a coincidence that this minor one-man crusade to revive hurling — a forerunner of a similar major one a year later — was made in the issues of the *Shamrock* for February and March. By then either Cusack had stopped attending DHC committee meetings, or else none were being held for him to attend. Moreover, his 1883 campaign in *Shamrock* ended just before the final committee meeting early in April. This we know he did attend, supporting the decision to suspend practice matches indefinitely, thus effectively winding up the DHC.

Some years later when the GAA was firmly established, Cusack boasted that in 1883 he turned his back on 'the foreign faction'. In fact he was to have many contacts with all sections of the athletics fraternity until the late summer of 1884 — almost invariably, however, in order to further his campaign for a new Irish sports body. However, his use of the *Shamrock* to publicise his views was an attempt to broaden his appeal. It represented a deliberate decision to try to reform Irish athletics from outside the existing system by canvassing nationalist support outside Dublin.

In the 17 February issue of the *Shamrock*, after a passing reference to hurling in an essay on physical education, came an invitation to his young male readers to 'get up hurling clubs'. A week later he told them of the recent foundation of the DHC 'for the revival of the old Irish game of hurling'. On 10 and 17 March he devoted the whole of his weekly article to various aspects of hurling, emphasising its antiquity and convincingly arguing that when played properly it was not dangerous.

Recalling that the old game of bowling (which a century later still survives in Cork) had been suppressed by the police, he warned that the same fate could befall hurling. He dealt in detail with the skills required of a good hurler, and ended with a survey of the historical accounts of hurling from BC 1272 — some 600 years before the first Olympics, he proudly pointed out. Apart from a promise on 23 June to treat hurling seriously again later, no other references to the game were made in the *Shamrock* until 1884.

For the moment, at least until the end of the athletics season permitted a return to hurling, it was back to the track for Cusack. The months of May and June found him at three popular sports meetings; at each he made his presence felt in a different way. Moreover, the press comments that followed two of these events gave some idea of what Cusack was up to that summer.

First, in mid-May, he attended the DAC meeting at Lansdowne Road. Significantly, however, for an event sponsored by a club of which he was now a committee member, he was content to be a spectator rather than a competitor or judge. A cryptic comment followed in the next athletics notes of *Sport*: 'On dit that a certain well known "hurler on the ditch" ... is about organising another meeting over the same ground.' A month later he was back at the same venue; this time he competed, taking second place for the second year in succession to Harte in the 16 lb weight event.

Between these two appearances Cusack made the long trip to the prestigious Cork city annual sports, where he not only caused a disturbance but also suffered a personal rebuff from which he was still smarting a year later. Beaten into second place in the 56 lb weight event, he lost an objection to the winner, who (Cusack claimed) by accepting prize money had lost his amateur status. In the 16 lb event Cusack was judged to have used an improper weight. A bitter press controversy over these two incidents followed between Cusack and the secretary of the sponsoring Cork Amateur Athletic Club, J. F. O'Crowley. The most interesting detail to emerge from this was an accusation by O'Crowley that the real purpose of 'the Gaelic champion' in visiting Cork was to further his 'Gaelic mission'. This charge Cusack ignored, as he proceeded to attack his opponent in intemperate language that cannot have won much new support for any mission he may have visited Cork for.

From these admittedly sparse accounts of Cusack's activities that summer two impressions emerge, if somewhat vaguely. First, one sees dimly the beginnings of the fusion of his ideas on reform of athletics with his dream of a hurling revival — the twin approach that, near the end of 1884, was to lead to the Gaelic Athletic Association, with its dual aims for athletics and Gaelic games. Secondly, however, one senses that Cusack's impetuous approach was still getting him nowhere. Indeed, his brusque and often pugnacious manner made him unpopular even among some non-unionist athletes, while many (but not all) of the unionist athletes regarded him as little more than a crank.

The athletics season had not yet concluded when Cusack made the first of two journeys out of Dublin in the summer and autumn of 1883 to further the cause of the Irish language. On 1 July he took a leading part in an excursion to the ancient monastic site of Monasterboice in Louth, where his was the only speech made in Irish.[1] Nearly three months later, in mid-September, he travelled to Belfast with another member of the Gaelic Union to re-organise the Union's branch in that city. By then too he was busily, indeed industriously, preparing for a forthcoming meeting between a deputation from the Union and the Education Commissioners, the ultimate failure of which was to provoke in 1884 one of Cusack's liveliest ever campaigns in the nationalist press.

Even before his visit to Belfast, however, Cusack had resumed hurling sessions in the Phoenix Park. On a Saturday afternoon early in September with three others — almost certainly the brothers

Paddy and Tom Molohan from Clare and L. C. Slevin from Armagh — he began what was to be an unbroken weekly practice for almost eight months. By the end of that period Dublin had two new hurling clubs, and support for the long-neglected game of hurling was spreading in several parts of the country.

So confident had Cusack grown by the spring of 1884 that, given proper organisation, hurling could be revived on a countrywide basis that he spent the summer of that year canvassing influential support for a body to control and promote the game. This new mood of optimism had been inspired by the astonishing public support for the weekly two-hour sessions in the Phoenix Park.

The contrast between the DHC practices in the spring of 1883, and those in the autumn of 1883, organised by Cusack alone, could hardly have been greater. From the start in September onlookers (who, it will be recalled, had been excluded by the DHC) were invited to join in. Within a few weeks not only strangers but students from Cusack's Academy — who now, incidentally dubbed him 'the Captain' — were participating in growing numbers. Nor did these, so far unorganised, 'metropolitan hurlers' venture on to the exclusive Polo Grounds; they were content with the flat but rougher sod close to the Wellington monument. Amongst the earliest of the spectators to take up a *camán* — probably one of the surplus sticks left over from the now defunct DHC — was a Tipperary man named J.K. Bracken, who was destined to be one of the founders of the GAA fourteen months later.

'The experiments in the Phoenix Park,' wrote Cusack over thirty years later, 'proved successful and attractive.'[2] Nevertheless, presumably to increase audience participation, in October (only weeks after the sessions had begun) he formed Cusack's Academy Hurling Club. For two more months matches between the students and the visitors continued. By then the latter were numerous enough and skilled enough to form a second club, so at a meeting held in Cusack's Academy at 4 Gardiner's Place on 5 December 1883 he founded the Metropolitan Hurling Club. Inside a year, as Cusack put it in 1887, the Metropolitans were the club 'out of which the GAA sprang'.[3]

Of the identity of the original members of the 'Mets', as this club came to be called, little is known, mainly because it received little notice in the Dublin newspapers — indeed, practically none from the nationalist publications. From the first few meetings only eight surnames have survived — Gardiner, Geary, Gibbs, Martin,

Molohan (which of the two brothers is not clear), Munton, Richer and Travers. Gibbs, formerly a prominent member of the Civil Service Athletic Club, had been a hurley player; Molohan, who became the Mets' first team captain, was from Clare, and either he or a brother continued to play hurley with the High School team.

From reports of the Mets' activities in the following couple of years one can add the surnames of seventeen more players — Barrett, Bolger, Cross, Harrison, Holmes, Kennedy, Kenny, Lyons, McGarvey, O'Callaghan, O'Mullane, O'Shea, Potterton (2), Purcell, Scully (or Sully) and Tickell. This total of twenty-four names (twenty-six when Cusack and Slevin are added) supports two boasts of Cusack about the Mets — that its members came from 'every creed' and from all parts of the country. Specifically, it is known that Kennedy came from Wexford, Kenny from Limerick, McGarvey from Donegal, the Pottertons from Armagh, Holmes from Down, Cross from Tyrone, Lyons from Westmeath, O'Shea from Tipperary, and Purcell and O'Mullane from Cork. Many were civil servants.

Although, as several of the surnames suggest, Cusack had attracted some Protestants into the Mets, the break with the DHC was almost complete. Only two former DHC members appear to have joined the Mets, the brothers Frank and Robert Potterton from Newry, whose acquaintance with Cusack probably went back to his period in that town in the early 1870s. Later, according to Cusack in 1887, some members of the Dublin Metropolitan Police force also joined.

The weekly sessions of the Mets' and Cusack's Academy hurlers continued every Saturday afternoon in the Phoenix Park, until Cusack suspended them in mid-June when the athletics season began, with the intention of resuming them later in the autumn. Amongst the city's sporting fraternity they attracted widespread interest and growing numbers of spectators. However, so far as the press was concerned, Cusack's latest venture got very little publicity and practically none at all from either of the two influential Home Rule papers, the daily *Freeman's Journal* and its weekly subsidiary *Sport*.

Before 1883 a bitter personal feud had developed between the proprietor of the *Freeman*, Edmund Dwyer Gray MP, and Cusack. Although the cause of this quarrel is unknown, the possibility that Gray resented Cusack's brusque, not to say aggressive, manner in his attempts to obtain publicity in Gray's papers for hurling cannot be ruled out; he later described Cusack as 'intolerable'.[4] This confrontation between the two was to have disastrous consequences for Cusack in 1886.

That Gray behaved unreasonably and insensitively towards Cusack is clear. The manager of *Sport*, Fred Gallagher, presumably on his employer's orders, instructed his editorial staff not to accept from Cusack any reports of hurling. Moreover, in March 1884 Gray extended the ban to the *Freeman* staff, and had Cusack barred from its offices permanently. This order the persistent Clareman apparently frustrated simply by meeting journalists in the commercial section of the premises, to which the public naturally had access.

According to Cusack there was a more sinister aspect to his quarrel with Gray. The *Freeman*, he claimed, wanted him to join its sporting staff so that he could not continue to write for the *Shamrock*, or even extend his contributions to the widely read *United Ireland*, edited by the immensely popular Home Rule figure, William O'Brien MP — something that did indeed happen in 1884. Although Cusack made this startling accusation publicly in 1887 when Gray was still alive, nobody ever refuted his charge on behalf of the *Freeman*.

However, like Cusack's unionist opponents then in charge of athletics in Dublin, the *Freeman* management under-estimated his determination and his considerable skill as a propagandist. For a start, in the early part of 1884 it became apparent that conditions were becoming gradually more favourable to the success of a campaign like that in which Cusack was engaged. Other amateur sports, rowing and cricket amont them, were also aiming at self-government. The popular weekly *Irish Sportsman*, which had opened its columns to Cusack back in 1881, suddenly began to take an interest in both Home Rule for athletics and the hurling revival. Internal evidence suggests that Cusack was still able to exploit an old friendship with the Dunbar family, which owned the paper.

An editorial article in the *Irish Sportsman* of 12 January 1884, which dealt at length with neglected national pastimes, expressly stated that the paper would favour the revival of hurling. Two weeks later another editorial dealt with the need for a body to govern Irish athletics; 'we need Home Rule in Irish athletics'; it ended. The same week an anonymous article on the current re-awakening of interest in hurling appeared in the *Dublin Sporting News*.

On 28 February, an anonymous reader of the *Irish Sportsman* from

Blackrock College (where Cusack presumably still had friends) argued the case for the restoration to sports programmes of weight and jumping events. On 12 April, in a special article on a forthcoming hurling match, the same paper stated that it had been watching with interest the hurling revival. Recalling the violence that had been associated with the game in rural areas until hurling had declined in the early part of the century, it stated that it was satisfied that as played under Cusack's management the game was free from physical dangers to participants.

From (of all places) London now came unexpected evidence of the impact of Cusack's hurling revival. Near the end of March 1884 a prestigious English periodical, *The Illustrated Sporting and Dramatic News,* published a whole page of drawings of Cusack and his hurlers at play in the Phoenix Park.[5] An associated article explained the rules of the game. The artist, a Tipperary man named Fitzgerald, had been touring Ireland for several months, and his laudatory account of hurling is in striking contrast with an illustrated account of an Irish cricket game which he also attended; this ended in a bout of fisticuffs.

Easily the most effective weapon, however, used by Cusack in the first half of 1884 to advance his views on both athletics and hurling was the weekly issue of the *Shamrock* magazine. Between 12 January and 12 July he dealt with hurling in twelve issues and with athletics in eight, often covering both topics in the same article. The longest contributions appeared under the title of 'Hurling' or 'Athletics', but in addition both subjects were cleverly introduced into his students' column when he was replying to queries or commenting on work sent in to him for correction or advice.

Both the tone and the length of these articles varied considerably from week to week. One week he was content to slip in one short sentence; the next he would publish a lengthy essay, varying from a persuasive style to blunt invective. The intention of the series as a whole was to arouse interest in the game of hurling and to canvass support for a new system of government for athletics, both aims to be achieved by a new body controlled by nationalists, but open to anybody sympathetic to national pastimes. Events later that same year suggest that Cusack achieved his aim. 'The articles in the *Shamrock* prepared the country for what was to follow,' he recalled many years later.[6]

The first four issues in January and February, dealing with hurling, twice explained the rise of the Mets. Four issues in March analysed in some detail the game of hurling, giving advice on playing styles, the ideal types of stick and ball, and on how to avoid injury, as well as urging schools and colleges to take up the game. Finally, two more issues, early in April and in May, covered several related topics — how to start clubs, reports on a hurling match in Ballinasloe (soon to be dealt with), with references to the game spreading outside Dublin as evidenced by reports and letters reaching Cusack.

On athletics, Cusack began his campaign on the 24 January issue of the *Shamrock* with a scathing criticism on the then common omission from programmes of traditional Irish events. A week later he explained the restrictive effect of a too rigid interpretation of the amateur rule, recalling his 1882 success with the DAC. 'For years ... clubs excluded ... police, soldiers, mechanics and other people who are vulgar enough to be muscular and ... would give a daddy-long-legs ... no chance ... in the presence of his wasp-waisted sweetheart.'

On 9 February, he quoted with approval a recent *Irish Sportsman* article criticising the state of athletics, and pointed to a decision by the amateur rowing body to widen its definition of amateur status. It was seven weeks later before he again concentrated on athletics; on 29 March he welcomed the forthcoming Caledonian Games to be staged in Dublin. Two months later he returned to his favourite theme of traditional Irish athletic events, taking the opportunity also to urge the spread of athletics outside Dublin.

In the middle of Cusack's *Shamrock* campaign of 1884 came a surprise (and to him a welcome) development. From south Galway, where hurling had survived and several clubs existed, came an invitation to the Metropolitans to play the Killimor team in Ballinasloe on Easter Monday. A ten-sovereign silver trophy was specially donated by two prominent local businessmen, and a train was chartered to bring the visitors from Dublin.

A big crowd turned up at Ballinasloe Fair Green — too many, indeed, for comfort, for spectators apparently continually encroached on to the pitch. Despite prior agreement on the rules of play, the game itself proved a disappointment. It ended abruptly when the home team scored and Cusack called off his men on the pretext that their opponents were too rough; in a Dublin newspaper, which would hardly have been read in Ballinasloe, he alleged that they 'slashed in a reckless and savage manner'.[7] However, each side then gave an exhibition of its style, and pony races and athletic contests (in which latter Cusack successfully participated) brought the unusual occasion to a close. Killimor naturally claimed victory, although when it came to a race for the free beer provided for the rival hurlers the Mets (presumably led by their captain) easily won.[8]

Notwithstanding the unsatisfactory nature of the hurling contest, the Mets' visit to the West had several important consequences. It encouraged the formation of other hurling clubs around the country, although exactly where Cusack did not specify, except to make it clear that the total had grown since March. It focussed attention on the urgent need for standard rules, which only a generally accepted national body could sponsor, thus strengthening Cusack's case for such a body. Two months later another challenge match was played in Ballinasloe, this time between two Galway clubs. Despite the existence of what were known as the Killimor Rules, both teams this time agreed to play under the rules introduced at Easter by Cusack's men from Dublin, a decision that indicates Cusack's growing status as the leader of the hurling revival movement.

The *Shamrock* was by no means the only publication which published regular contributions by Cusack in the first half of 1884. Besides running his Academy (with outstanding success that year), conducting what amounted to a weekly correspondence course in the *Shamrock,* and attending most of the weekly meetings of the Gaelic Union, he also engaged in a fierce public controversy with the Commissioners of Education over the right of children from Irish-speaking homes to what he (and the Union) felt was the most suitable language of instruction in the national schools in their areas. This prolonged, and almost entirely one-sided, epistolatory offensive was a direct result of the refusal of the educational authorities to give the Gaelic Union an opportunity to air their grievances at an oral hearing. Without seeking the Union's backing, Cusack took it on himself to engage the Education Commissioners in battle on his own, and far from being in the least daunted by the customary bureaucratic reaction — indifferent, if not contemptuous, silence — continued to mount a blistering attack on them over a period of four months.

Between 1 March and 28 June 1884 Cusack had at least one letter a week on the subject of the Irish language in the national schools published in one or more of the three nationalist weeklies, the *Nation,* the *Irishman* and *United Ireland.* On several occasions Cusack's letter occupied the greater part of a page of tiny print, and none of those involved in the controversy — the Commissioners, the training professors, the teachers — escaped stinging (and at times abusive) criticism. The details of this episode are largely irrelevent to an account of Michael Cusack, the athletics reformer and hurling revivalist, except in one respect: they provide impressive evidence of his intellectual capacity. His incisive style, his ability to marshal statistics, his knowledge and ingenious exploitation of more liberal British educational policies in other parts of the world they ruled, and his use of his own wide experience of primary education all combine to give a picture of a brilliant mind. Had his many opponents in the world of sports then or in later years even cursorily read these letters, they would have hesitated before taking on Cusack in any controversy.

3

Early in the summer of 1884, when the new athletics season opened in Dublin and the provinces, Cusack again changed the tactics of his one-man campaign. At sports meetings in widely scattered parts of the country he made the case in person for reform of athletics, specifically urging the setting up of a new sports body to govern athletics. Amongst the places he is believed to have visited for this purpose are Monasterevan, Gorey, Tralee and Limerick. This lobbying lasted at least until the end of July. Then in August came a significant break-through in his campaign, which at last gave real hope of success.

Even during the summer months, however, Cusack did not entirely abandon the written word. On the contrary, he found several opportunities to report on the progress of his campaign, or to give the impression (correctly, as it now seems) that support for it was increasing around the country. In mid-April one of his rare letters to the *Irish Times* expressed confidence that, despite the anti-patriotic sentiments he knew existed, the 'old games' would soon be revived 'in every village and town where the Celtic element prevails'.[9] Just over a month later he claimed that reports were reaching him of a hurling revival during the previous few months. Twice in June he openly boasted that events were moving in the direction he desired. In the *Shamrock* he indicated on 14 June that plans were in train for a new Irish athletics body, and a week later in the *Irish Sportsman* of 21 June he remarked that Irish athletics were being 'thoroughly revived' just then.

Why, one may ask, after several months making the case for a hurling revival did he now switch to athletics? There is an obvious explanation. With the start of the new athletics season it became clear that his opponents in the leading athletic clubs had begun to make a concerted effort to introduce into the country from England the regime of the Amateur Athletic Association. The AAA had gained its first foothold here in 1882 with the affiliation of the Ulster Cricket Club, and in 1883 Trinity Athletic Club's annual sports were controlled by the AAA. By 1884 more and more local meetings were being held under AAA rules, and it became obvious that if Cusack's opponents had their way this would be their alternative to his plan to win Home Rule for Irish athletics.

Just how serious the unionist-dominated clubs were became apparent at the first big meeting of the 1884 season in Dublin, a unique sporting event in which Cusack played a prominent part. At Whit the Scots community for the first time held their own Caledonian Games, with events normally seen only at meetings in the Highlands dominating the programme. Advance publicity and the novelty of the occasion attracted a crowd of over 20,000 to Lansdowne Road. The games were staged again in 1885 and 1886, but on a smaller scale and with less success than in 1884.

Exploiting a friendship with the leader of the Caledonian Society of Ireland, a journalist and publisher named Morrison Miller, Cusack joined in the organisation of the Games and was praised in the press reports for his efforts. He cannot, however, have regarded the Games as an unqualified success, for the AAA (under whole rules the meeting was run) refused to recognise three events — the 22 lb shot, the tug-of-war and the 21 lb hammer. To avoid a confrontation, to save athletes the risk of suspension and doubtless also to challenge the AAA, these events were run off before the rest of the programme, a ruse one suspects Cusack may have had a hand in.

Not for the first or last time, however, his opponents under-estimated Cusack's fighting spirit. Almost at once he took the fight into their camp and got revenge for the AAA's action at the Caledonian Games in down-grading events he was campaigning to have restored to programmes. Returning briefly to the Dublin Athletics Club, now the sponsors of the annual championship meeting in succession to the defunct ICAC, he succeeded in having the events, which had been banned from the Caledonian Games, restored after a lapse of several years to the championship meeting due to be held in mid-July. The public announcement by the DAC of this decision is unmistakably in Cusack's style; the events restored had, it stated, 'undoubted status as purely national pastimes in which the Irish have always maintained their supremacy.'

Back in Lansdowne Road only a month after the Caledonian Games, this time in the role of a sports reporter for the Home Rule weekly *United Ireland,* Cusack was disgusted by what he saw passing as Ireland's premier sports meeting, held under AAA rules. From his vantage-point inside the track he was appalled by the poor judging, the prominence given to the foot races he detested, and above all the arrogance of the bookmakers. A noisy scene developed as he loudly criticised the organisers, who tried to eject him and (according to Cusack) insulted his wife, who was with him. But he had not done his cause much good.

By now Cusack was coming to the conclusion that Dublin would never play a major role in his projected sports body. Increasingly, he began to concentrate on the provinces, where the indications were that support for his ideas was growing. Indeed, why he had not thought of this strategy earlier is a mystery. Perhaps the explanation is simply that in those days of slow travel, long before the era of the motor-car, he literally could not afford to spend time out of Dublin, away from his school and his family.

This new emphasis by Cusack on the provinces — which, after all, he had begun with his *Shamrock* articles earlier that year — took two forms. First he succeeded in having eight short anonymous articles prominently inserted in the weekly review (entitled 'What's Up') on the front page of *United Ireland.* These were intended mainly to persuade athletics organisers outside Dublin to take control of their own meetings, but also to show Cusack's opponents in Dublin that athletics need not necessarily be controlled from that city.

Next, he contacted prominent figures around the provinces, either personally or by letter (or both), on whom he felt he could rely. What he obviously had in mind here was to build up a network of support in areas where athletics flourished, so that when in due course he set up a national body local branches would appear at once in the areas he had contacted. These would, he naturally hoped, be led by the people he had canvassed in each area. Thanks to his foresight and planning, this is precisely what happened in 1885.

The first *United Ireland* article on 14 June was critical of 'those who are indefatigable in their efforts to steer our athletic meetings on the lines laid down by English promoters'. A week later he called for a 'manlier tone' in Irish athletics, and specifically argued that the Tralee sports of 17 June had shown that, except occasionally for foot races, handicapping was not needed if meetings were fairly conducted.

Then in the issue for 28 June came unmistakable evidence of how Cusack's campaign was taking shape, and also the first of several hints that he was planning a body based on Cork city. 'A new athletic club is to be formed ... We hope that ... those who are making a new move in the direction of reviving athletics in the capital of Munster will be careful to make their sports ... Irish in their character ... The advocates of foot races ... ought ... to allow the advocates of pure athletics to reintroduce the weights and jumps.'

A week later, on 5 July, Cusack again attacked those who wanted Irish athletics to be run under English standards — whose 'guiding rule', he had alleged on 28 June, 'was to keep off their programmes ... every event at which Irishmen can beat Englishmen, and put on every event at which Englishmen can beat us.' The AAA, he pointed out, was merely a self-constituted body with arbitrary rules. Promoters of Irish sports who supported this system degraded Irish athletes. Explaining that, of the 103 delegates at an AAA general meeting, only two (from an Ulster cricket club) were Irish, he suggested that 'Irishmen ought to know how to throw a weight or take a jump' without guidance from London.

The remaining four *United Ireland* paragraphs were partly propagandist and partly critical in character. On 12 July, in an article written largely in humorous vein, he gave an account of the recent annual championship meeting in Dublin; by comparison, an editorial article in that same week's issue of the *Irishman,* also ummistakably from Cusack's pen, dealt with the same event in a more serious tone. The 2 August issue of *United Ireland* found him praising the *Freeman's Journal* for its support of its staff's athletic activities — possibly a subtle attempt to win over this important Dublin club, with its obvious nationalist associations, to his campaign.

That Cusack's contributions to *United Ireland* were being widely read outside Dublin is evident from his boast on 28 June that his earlier suggestion for less rigid handicapping had been accepted by the organisers of the Limerick sports meeting on 21 June. However, on 23 August in his final article he found it necessary to return to this topic, alleging that much of the handicapping he had recently seen was dishonest. The previous week he had compared unfavourably the management of the 5 July Lansdowne Road event with the many meetings in the provinces, where weight and jump events had returned to prominence and where, he believed, 'athletics were in a far more flourishing condition than ever since the so-called revival . . . eighteen years ago.'

As to Cusack's personal contacts with local groups in the provinces, until 1984 the Loughrea meeting of mid-August 1884 was the only evidence of Cusack's campaign in the summer of that year. Moreover, because of both the lack of documentation and the unsatisfactory accounts that have survived, this meeting was at best a shaky foundation for suggesting the existence of any such contacts. However, the discovery just 100 years after it was written of a hitherto unknown letter from Cusack to Maurice Davin at last allows the Loughrea meeting to fall into context.

According to local tradition, the background to the Loughrea meeting was a friendship that had developed some five years earlier, in the house of a common acquaintance in Dublin, between Cusack and William J. Duffy of Loughrea. As a result of a renewal of contacts between the two, a delegation of local athletics or hurling enthusiasts met Bishop Duggan of Clonfert in his home in the town of 15 August 1884. They informed him of their plans for a new sports body and asked his support. Although sympathetic, he pleaded ill-health and urged them instead to approach Archbishop Croke of Cashel.[10]

Unfortunately, none of the participants left any record of this meeting, so that one is wholly dependent on oral accounts handed down to later generations. To make matters worse, these local folk memories differ in some important details. For instance, it is not even certain if Cusack was present, or merely came from Dublin at Duffy's urging and met only the local men. This latter version suggests that after a preliminary discussion in a local house he decided not to accompany the party to the bishop's house nearby.

Apart from the date and the purpose of the meeting, the only other agreed fact is that the core of the delegation comprised Duffy, John P. McCarthy and John Sweeney (all of Loughrea) and Peter Kelly and Michael Glennon (from east Galway). There is also disagreement on the role played by a fourth Loughrea man, Martin Egan. Because he was intimate with Duggan, it is thought that he may have arranged the meeting.

Almost incredibly, neither Cusack nor any of the Loughrea men acted on the bishop's suggestion to approach Croke. Equally curious, despite his close connections with that part of Galway, Cusack himself never subsequently referred to the meeting either. Moreover, a biographer of Bishop Duggan, who wrote at a time when many of the participants must still have been alive, made no reference to the 1884 meeting, although he did record the significant fact that as a young man the bishop had been a notable athlete.

The credentials of the Loughrea men to head a Galway or Connacht section of a nationalist-controlled sports body were impeccable. All had Land League or Fenian connections, or both. Kelly five years later was to become a GAA president at a time when the Association was dominated by the IRB. Duffy had two periods as secretary of the Galway county board of the GAA as well as being an Irish Party MP for many years. All were reputed to be associates of P. W. Nally (now 'on the run' because of his Fenian activities), whose views on the reform of athletics Bishop Duggan is also likely to have fully shared.

4

The Gaelic Union,
4 Gardiner's Place,
Dublin.

26th August, 1884

Dear Mr. Davin:

The Irish Association with its rules etc. must be formed before the end of the year. The Association could organise the whole country within the year 1885. We could then safely hold the projected mass gathering in 1886. The business must be worked from Munster.

Suppose we held a meeting of delegates in some central place in Tipperary on the first of November next? Don't bother your head about Dublin. The place couldn't well be worse than it is. We'll have to look to the provinces for men. Dublin will have to fall in or keep up the connection with England.

I have written to Cork this day telling them that you have responded most heartily. I am sure Mr. Stack of Listowel will look after North Kerry. Although I am not a member of the National League I think I am not without influence with several of its leading members. The National Press will give me room for squibs when I am ready. 'The Shamrock' is also at my disposal. I hope to see it enlarged in about a month and then the education of the people could start in earnest. The paragraphs on athletics in 'United Ireland' are exploding like shells in the enemy ranks. Of course they know it's my doing and that therefore the paper is not likely to hang fire soon.

I have found it to be utterly hopeless to revive our national pastimes without the assistance of the leaders of the people and I have not hesitated to urge my claims on them with a persistence that brooks no refusal. After a protracted struggle I won all round. Our business now is to work together, caring for none but the Irish people and quietly shoving aside all who would denationalise these people.

I'll write to you again when business is a little further advanced.

> With many thanks,
> Yours faithfully,
> Michael Cusack.

The letter reproduced above, which was discovered in Davin's home a hundred years to the month after it was written, sheds new light on the foundation of the GAA, and especially on the events leading up to it. Hitherto it had been assumed, for lack of evidence to the contrary, that Maurice Davin first appeared on the scene only after Cusack's famous anonymous article 'A Word About Irish Athletics' in two of the nationalist weeklies on 11 October 1884. This letter establishes that the two had been in touch for about two months before that, and almost certainly for much longer also.

The Cusack letter establishes at least two other important facts. Up to now it has been widely suspected that the Thurles meeting of 1 November 1884, at which the GAA was formally founded, was a hurried last-minute affair. The small attendance and the absence of any speedy following-up action led to this belief. The letter, however, unmistakably shows Cusack planning for a meeting on 1 November 'in some central place in Tipperary'.

The second important fact proved by Cusack's letter is that the writer had established contact with influential people around the provinces, who would take the initiative in their areas when he set up the new body. By clear implication he already had support in Cork (probably the city); he was also satisfied that North Kerry was safely on his side. 'Mr Stack of Listowel' was, of course, William Moore Stack, a leading Kerry Fenian and father of Austin Stack, the future Kerry footballer and Sinn Féin leader. Stack senior effectively founded the GAA in Kerry in 1885; Stack junior became a Minister in the first Dáil Government in 1919.

Not surprisingly, Cusack also had a nucleus of support in Dublin, mostly associates of the Metropolitan Hurling Club who were to play a role in the events of the two months after the letter to Davin. With the knowledge of the existence of these three groups (in Cork, Kerry and Dublin) the Loughrea meeting of 15 August 1884 can be taken to show that an East Galway group also flourished. Precisely how many more such informal groups Cusack had succeeded in setting up elsewhere is not known. However, both the attendance at the Thurles meeting on 1 November 1884 and local tradition in both countries would point to the existence of support for him too in counties Tipperary and Kilkenny.

The importance of Davin's adherence to Cusack's movement — his 'hearty response' — can hardly be exaggerated. In all probability it was the turning-point for Cusack, the one influential source or type of support he needed to be reasonably certain of success. Although by then retired from active participation in athletics, the powerfully-built Tipperary man had for some twenty years been in every sense a towering figure in Irish athletics. The oldest of four talented brothers (one of whom lived on into the 1940s) whose prowess at sports meetings had gone back almost to the start of the modern revival in the mid-1860s, he had achieved international repute by defeating leading British rivals even on their home tracks.

Moreover, Davin had for many years put as much back into Irish athletics as he had taken out of it. Although residing in an area remote from most venues for major meetings, he acted as judge at many of them. He had also shown an active interest in improving the system of government of Irish athletics, and at least seven years before 1884 had advocated one all-Ireland body to control athletics generally, to improve standards and to standardise practices at meetings.[11]

At the personal level, Davin also had two assets which Cusack lacked. In the first place, although of modest, indeed almost retiring, demeanour, he was immensely popular with all sections of the Irish sporting public. In addition, although a committed nationalist — who, incidentally, like Cusack, had in all probability been a Fenian in his youth — Davin was an orthodox Home Ruler. As such he would have been much more acceptable to unionists than the bombastic Clareman, who was given frequently to suggesting (quite wrongly) that he was an advocate of physical force.

With the capture of Davin, Cusack also found a leader for his proposed new body — at least a titular leader, but much more too, as the next five years were to show. It is to Cusack's credit that he realised that he himself was not made of the stuff that makes leaders.[12] There is little doubt that he was content to be the pioneer with the ideas, which he left to others less abrasive than him to put into practice. The humble roles he was glad to play in the GAA for the last twenty years of his life demonstrated his total lack of ambition — if not of rancour for the direction 'his' Association took for most of that period.

The apparently unqualified nature of Davin's response to Cusack's approach implies that both were in agreement not merely on the need for a new sports body but also on at least the general form it should take. However, in the absence of Cusack's previous (or first?) letter to Davin and of the latter's response (to which Cusack's 26 August letter was a reply), it is unclear if at this early stage the two envisaged a body to cater for athletics only or one to control both it and hurling. Furthermore, despite Cusack's use of the phrase 'our national pastimes', it appears that football only found a place on his programme at Davin's suggestion — perhaps insistence.

Amongst other facts which the 26 August letter reveals is that there was still no fixed title for the new body. The title of Munster Athletic Club, referred to in his memoirs by Davin's brother, Pat, had now given way to the broader title of the Irish Association. At this stage Cork was obviously still preferred as the location of the headquarters of the new body. Moreover, while Cusack may have found a leader for his body in the person of Davin, we know from Cusack that the search for a patron had not yet begun — despite Bishop Duggan's advice of mid-August 1884. As the second-last sentence shows, his overriding aim still was to frustrate the plans of those who, by imposing the AAA regime on Irish athletics, would make this country a satellite of England in outdoor sports.

Around the time he was concentrating on winning Maurice Davin to his cause, Cusack was also canvassing support from Home Rule and Land League leaders. The 26 August letter indicates that he had been forced to conclude that without such support his movement would not succeed. It also claims that after making his case persistently he had succeeded with the leaders he had approached.

With the exception of the Land League founder, Michael Davitt, with whom he had then a cordial relationship, one may doubt whether in this part of his letter Cusack was telling the whole truth. Three different statements of his — in 1887, 1888 and 1889 — agree on Davitt's promise of support.[13] In the Catholic Club in Dublin in August 1884, the two had discussed Cusack's plans, and Davitt (who had served seven years of a fifteen-year sentence in the 1870s for Fenian activities) claimed that he had conceived the idea of such a body while in jail. He approved of Cusack's proposal and promised to help him to set up an independent Irish athletic association. The reference in Cusack's letter to Davin to 'the projected mass gathering in 1886' shows that it was then that Davitt first put forward the idea of the revived Tailteann Games, an idea for which Cusack always gave him credit.

However, the extent and nature of the commitment of the Home Rule leaders is far from clear, despite the widespread support Cusack's new body received at grass-roots level. Parnell, he later admitted, he did not approach until after the GAA was founded. On the other hand, it can be assumed that the statement in the invitation to the Thurles meeting of 1 November, that Justin McCarthy MP and Tim Harrington MP had given their approval, was correct. McCarthy's concern for the decline in national pastimes is known, and Harrington would have been quick to deny Cusack's claim when some months later he fell out with Cusack.

As for Tim Healy MP and Tom Sexton MP, two other prominent figures in the Irish Party whom he had got to know through his work for the Irish language, it is a curious fact that Cusack never claimed to have sought backing from either. In Healy's case it would certainly have been forthcoming, something one cannot be sure of in Sexton's, for he was closely involved in the management of the *Freeman's Journal* and would have known of the Gray-Cusack feud. The support of William O'Brien MP can be taken for granted, if only because he had already allowed Cusack to use the columns of *United Ireland,* of which he was the editor. However, the failure of the *Nation* to publish Cusack's seminal 11 October article suggests that despite his admiration for the Sullivan family (who controlled that paper) he failed to win its support. The sudden death in October of A. M. Sullivan may have been a factor in this failure.

Since the next known public move by Cusack after his 26 August letter to Davin was the 11 October article in *United Ireland* and the *Irishman,* it has to be admitted that nothing is known of his activities for the whole of September 1884. With the athletic season in Dublin closing at the end of August, the number of meetings in the provinces would presumably have gradually tailed-off during September. It seems unlikely that he spent much, or indeed any, of that month outside Dublin. There does not appear to have been any pretext for a journey out of the capital on Gaelic Union business, such as had probably accounted for an otherwise unexplained visit to Belfast in July.

Since the letter to Davin indicates that he was not yet ready to make the final move in the national press, Cusack must have still had some loose ends to tie up, or some lobbying to do, in September. The letter ends with a promise to write to Davin again 'when business is a little further advanced', and it can be assumed that a later letter (now lost) did make arrangements for Davin to reply publicly to Cusack's article when it appeared. There remains the possibility that in September Cusack returned to Cork, which until well into October was still being considered (by him at least) as the location for the headquarters of his new body.

Three fragments of information suggest that Cusack was not idle in Dublin in September. That month the Mets resumed their Saturday sessions, which continued to the end of the year, by which time the club had become the first to join the new Association. That Cusack was still trying to spread hurling in Dublin is suggested by the appearance in October of a third club, the Dublin Workingmen's Hurling Club, based at Christchurch Place. Furthermore, since by mid-October at the latest he had divulged his plans for a new national body to a group of his closest intimates on the Mets committee — J.J. Kenny, Martin Kelly and Michael Hegarty in particular — tactics and prospects must have been fully discussed in September also.[14]

The sub-leader, 'A Word About Irish Athletics', in the two weekly nationalist organs (*United Ireland* and *Irishman*) of 11 October 1884 was beyond doubt the most effective single piece of writing Cusack ever did. By the standards of the average editorial article in such a paper of that time, it was neither long nor diffuse. Running only to some 700 words, it was tightly constructed and bears signs of careful composition, even for a master of the English language like Cusack. Cleverly planned and logically thought out, it is entirely free from the invective which he frequently resorted to when roused by opposition or hostility. He was justifiably proud of it for the rest of his life.[15]

Cusack's thesis was simple. National pastimes, he argued, were an essential element of a thriving nation, and any neglect of them usually began in urban areas. Not only had this been happening in Ireland, but the rot was now also starting to spread to the provinces. The reason for this decline, he believed, was because Irish athletics were controlled by people hostile to national aspirations. Accordingly, the time had come for the masses to take control of their own pastimes and to draft rules for this purpose.

To the reader over one hundred years later, Cusack's outlook may seem racialist and chauvinistic in places, even, as it must have seemed in the eyes of Dublin Castle, provocatively seditious in its linkage of physical fitness to warlike qualities. It bluntly castigates 'the hostile laws of a hated ... dominant race', and clearly implies that current English fashions in sport, which included 'betting and flagrant cheating' were not merely alien (in every sense) to Irish cirumstances but also morally degrading.

However, criticism of this kind is to judge popular nationalist opinion of a century ago by the standards of the 1980s. What Cusack was enunciating was just one tenet of the nationalist creed of his day, accepted by all non-unionist factions. Moreover, considering the high political temperature of the time his tone is relatively moderate and comparatively balanced — if not restrained, for that (for good or ill) was not Cusack's nature. No doubt, he was conscious of his success in having won converts from the unionist camp whom he hoped — indeed, had some reason to believe — would support a new Irish-based atheltics body.

To the great majority of the readers of the two papers that published Cusack's article, it was an emotional but cleverly-argued attempt to rouse those concerned about the future of Irish athletics and games. More importantly, to the members of the various groups around the provinces to whom Cusack had confided his plans — in Cork, Galway, Kerry, Tipperary and doubtless other places where folk memories are now dimmed or secrets were carefully kept — it was both a signal of impeding action and a call for support.

For his longer-established circle of younger readers Cusack gave an even clearer message in the *Shamrock* of 11 October. 'We ... suggest ... the formation of a society for the preservation and cultivation of our national pastimes. Such a society could well be worked from Cork ... [its] athletic club ought to be a good nucleus for an association which should draw up rules for ... every description of Gaelic athletics ... Past and present champions [should] join hands ... and devise a movement for every form of pastime which found favour with ... the Celtic race.'

Right on cue, the other principal actor in Cusack's drama played his pre-arranged role. A week later the issue of 18 October of the first two papers carried an unequivocal offer of support in a letter from Maurice Davin. Compared to Cusack's article the week before, Davin's letter was short, to the point, highly individualist and low-key in its nationalist sentiments. Perhaps its contrasting style and tone made it all that much more effective.

It was time, urged the Tipperary athlete, that a rule-book for all Irish games was published, proceeding next to echo a frequent complaint of Cusack about the absence from sports programmes of weight and jumping events. Then, in a pointed sentence which drew attention to an omission from Cusack's article, Davin said bluntly that 'Irish football is a great game and worth going a long way to see when played ... under proper rules.' However, since there simply were no existing rules for either hurling or football, both games were often dangerous.

Warming to his subject, Davin said he was anxious to see both games revised, but only 'under regular rules'. Curiously, for a man known to the public mainly as an athlete, he made no reference to athletics — unless by games he meant to include them too. He disagreed with Cusack's attacks on harriers' clubs, which in Davin's view were 'a good means of bringing out long-distance runners'. Then he revealed obvious foreknowledge of Cusack's plans: 'the movement such as you advise is ... for the purpose of reviving Irish games and drafting rules ... I will gladly lend a hand if I can be of any use.'

'My friend Maurice Davin has spoken ... a leader spotless in the midst of the speckled,' began a short letter by Cusack (now out in the open for the first time in the series) in the issue of *United Ireland* for 25 October. As if to reassure Davin that they both had the same objects of their proposed revival in mind as national pastimes, he listed 'weights, jumps, hurling, Irish football, wrestling, bowling'. Athletics still came first in his priorities, which now included Irish football for the first time. For the record, wrestling (despite Cusack's apparent partiality for it) was destined to be outlawed from its games by the GAA soon after its foundation, and bowling (bowls as played in Cork today) was never seriously promoted by the GAA.

'In the event of a meeting being held to draft laws for the promotion ... of every form of Irish sport,' Cusack continued, he would 'offer advice humbly'. He then went on — either disingenuously or as a signal to his supporters in the provinces — to state that after talks he had had with representative figures, all had agreed that the proposal put forward by the paper (his own suggestion made anonymously) 'should at once be acted on'. The general feeling, he concluded, was for a meeting in Thurles on 1 November, and to that end a circular would be shortly issued to which he hoped there would be 'a response from those who desire to see genuine Irish athletics revived.'

A final letter from Cusack in *United Ireland* of 1 November served both as a last call for support and as a reminder. The circular (signed by himself and Davin) had, he claimed, brought 'a shower of replies'. The meeting aimed at 'inaugurating a movement which will be a means of providing rational and national amusements for the humbler and more neglected sections of our race' (an emphasis he was to repeat in the next few years) would be held that same day at 2 o'clock in the Commercial Hotel in Thurles.

Footnotes

1. *Irishman,* 7.7.1883 & 14.7.1883.
2. *Gaelic Athlete,* 7.3.1914.
3. *CT,* 2.4.1887.
4. *FJ,* 19.3.1886.
5. Vol. 21, 22.3.1884.
6. *Gaelic Athlete,* 7.3.1914.
7. *IT,* 15.4.1884.
8. For a Galway account, see P. O Laoi, *Annals of the GAA in Galway,* Vol. 1 (Galway, 1984) pp. 5-7.
9. 14.4.1884.
10. See sources referred to at footnote 25, Chapter One (p. 22) of de Búrca: *The GAA: A History* (Dublin, 1980); also O Laoi, op. cit., pp. 8 and 9.
11. *IS,* 3.11.1877.
12. *Camán,* 31.12.1932.
13. *CT,* 6.8.1887; *Chicago Citizen,* 22.9.1888; *Nation,* 6.7.1889; see also, undated letter of Cusack in *NLI,* MS 18, 560.

14. See *Republican File*, 28.11.1931.
15. *Nation*, 12.10.1889; *Gaelic Athlete*, 7.3.1914.

Principal Sources
Irish Sportsman, 1883 & 1884
Irishman, 1883 & 1884
United Ireland, 1884
Sport, 1884
Nation, 1884 & 6.7.1889
Freeman's Journal, 1884
Shamrock, 1883 & 1884
Irish Times, December 1883
Gaelic Athlete, 7.3.1914
Dublin University Athletic Union minute-book (TCD, MS 2257).
Davin, Pat: *Recollections of a Veteran Irish Athlete* (Dublin, 1938).

CHAPTER SIX
THE G.A.A. IS BORN
1844

The two years 1885 and 1886 were to be the most important in Michael Cusack's life, for it was then that the success or failure of the new departure he had planned for Irish sport would be decided. After his ten-year campaign for reform of organised outdoor sports, the meeting in Thurles now seemed likely to signal the rise of a body that would achieve his twin aims — the promotion of athletics by a body in which the majority nationalist community was fairly represented, and the revival by such a body of the ancient national game of hurling. Should this new organisation fail, however, Cusack would be merely an obscure figure in the history of modern Irish sport, and his ten years' work for Irish athletics would all have been in vain.

In the first three years of the GAA's life three major hurdles had, it transpired, to be crossed if the Association was to be a success; but at Thurles on 1 November 1884, Cusack can only have anticipated the first two. First, the shaky foundations laid in Hayes's Hotel had to be consolidated if the GAA was even to become a reality, a task which (as will shortly be argued) he barely achieved in the following two months. Secondly, the new organisation had to withstand what was certain to be determined opposition to its continued existence, by opponents with powerful support from across the Irish Sea, and soon to set up a rival body to Cusack's.

Had he been a shrewder observer of Irish politics, Cusack might have foreseen a third obstacle to be overcome before the body he had just founded could pay a major role in its chosen sphere of action. For no sooner had the GAA, more or less simultaneously, defeated the initial efforts to kill it off and taken firm root in the field of Irish sport, than it began to be coveted as the exclusive property of the two rival sections of the nationalist movement, the constitutional wing and the physical force wing.

Before this last development had reached its climax, however, Cusack had lost his dominant position in the GAA. For, notwithstanding all his imaginative and constructive ideas, when it

[Established over a Century.]

THE COMMERCIAL AND FAMILY HOTEL,

AND POSTING ESTABLISHMENT,

THURLES.

LIZZIE J. HAYES, Proprietress.

Hayes's Hotel, Thurles, as it was in the 1880s

came to the day-to-day running of a major organisation he lacked not only basic administrative skills but also essential qualities like leadership and tact. As a result, his associates were forced to conclude that the Association he had founded would only flounder under his continued rule. It was to be another ten years before Cusack was reconciled both to the GAA's role in nationalist affairs, and to the fact that he would never again enjoy an influential place in its councils.

As he travelled back by train to Dublin on the evening of 1 November 1884 all this dissension both inside and outside his new association still lay ahead of Cusack. For the moment an even more serious problem faced him — to ensure that the body he and Davin had founded earlier that day would remain in existence. The grim truth was that the meeting in Hayes's Hotel had almost been a flop, and that the GAA would indeed make no further impact on Irish sport unless it quickly got much more support than it had managed to muster in Thurles.

By three o'clock on 1 November only five people had joined Davin and Cusack in Lizzie Hayes's billards-room off the Square in Thurles. These were John Wyse Power, Joseph O'Ryan, John McKay, Joseph K. Bracken and Thomas St George McCarthy. Although understandably regarded ever since as the founders of the GAA, two of these seven (O'Ryan and McCarthy) never again took any part in the Association, and one of the two (McCarthy) was little more than a curious, and certainly a neutral, spectator at the foundation meeting.

After Davin had by agreement taken the chair — if indeed he literally did so, for some of the seven remained standing — Cusack read the convening circular. In a short statement Davin then summarised the case for a body to promote national pastimes, rather than continuing to accept a regime 'designed mainly for the guidance of Englishmen' and 'not ... at all ... characteristic ... of the Gaelic race'. Two longer speeches followed, one by Cusack which he ended by reading sixty messages of support he claimed to have received (or, more likely, the names of the sixty who had sent them), and the other by McKay, who called for a national athletic body which would not be bound by the rules of the Amateur Athletic Association (of England).

On Cusack's proposal Davin was elected president. Cusack, Power and McKay were elected secretaries, with power to add to their number — something incidentally (and probably regrettably, as events were to suggest) they never did. After agreeing to ask Croke, Parnell and probably Davitt — there being some doubt about the third — to become patrons, the meeting adjourned, so as to give the four elected officers time to draft rules for the new Association.

Such has been the long-term impact of this meeting, and yet so sparse the record of it, that within forty-eight hours myths began to grow about it, some of which are still accepted today, over a hundred years later. The first concerned the number who attended. This can now, it is suggested, be satisfactorily explained as a result of the chance discovery in Davin's home in 1984, along with Cusack's letter (already quoted) of August 1884, of a faded American press-cutting that Davin had preserved. This contained the vitriolic letter (also already referred to) that Cusack wrote to the *Chicago Citizen* almost four years after the Thurles meeting.[1]

A barbed remark in this Chicago letter shows that the newspapr reports of the Thurles meeting fall into two cateogories. One, emanating from Cusack or McKay and published in papers to which they had access (mainly the *Irishman, United Ireland* and the Cork city nationalist organs) lists seven names. The other report, written by a unionist journalist hostile to Cusack, based on hearsay and published in sources critical of him (among these the *Freeman* and the *Irish Sportsman*) names twelve people as having attended. This second account cannot be accepted as accurate.

Much of the confusion about precisely how many people got as far as Miss Hayes's billards-room was, it has to be admitted, caused by Cusack himself. By adding the cryptic and infuriating phrase 'etc, etc' to his authoritative list of seven, he gave a false impression that more than that number had attended. Moreover, inside two weeks he was claiming that the number was 'about a dozen'. For years, too, he continued to insist that Frank Maloney of Nenagh, who was undoubtedly in the vicinity of the hotel that day, also attended, something Maloney himself stated too.

That the proceedings in Thurles were intended to be merely a meeting about a meeting — and, but for Cusack's insistence, would not have got beyond that stage — is evident from two facts. One is the widely overlooked statement in the invitation that the venue for the meeting, instead of being Hayes's Hotel, would be a place to be decided there. The other is McKay's reluctance, which was accepted, to countenance the election of a committee. Clearly to him — and he took a major part in the proceedings — the meeting was to be of a purely exploratory nature. Twenty years later Cusack described the Hayes's Hotel proceeding as 'a rushed meeting', and in 1911 P.J. Devlin explained that it had been 'only a preliminary exchange of views'.[2]

The unrepresentative nature of the handful who actually attended the foundation meeting of the GAA shows how near it came to falling through altogether — just as the undoubted presence close by of another handful who stayed out of the billards-room suggests some disagreement about the meeting. Apart from Cusack, only two of the seven had come more than forty miles. One of these was McKay, the Belfast-born journalist then on the *Cork Examiner*, whose role in the infant GAA has, it is suggested, been hitherto understated. The other was John Wyse Power, an Irish-speaking Waterford-born journalist of mercurial temperament, then editing the Naas-based *Leinster Leader*. Power's important role in the early GAA — at least after Cusack had left its executive in 1886 — has, it is suggested, also been overlooked. That he was inactive for all of 1885 can be attributed to friction that developed early on between himself and Cusack.

McKay's role in the successful launching of the GAA may well indeed have been secondary only to that of Cusack and Davin. Cork and its athletic club appear for some months before November 1884 to have been central to Cusack's plans for his new association. It is no coincidence that McKay became a joint honorary secretary of the GAA, nor that Cork city was chosen as the venue for its second meeting. Admittedly for several months of 1885, even after the appearance of a rival association, McKay's club, the Cork AC, maintained an attitude of cautious neutrality between the GAA and its opponents. However, once he had given his unqualified support to the GAA it had fewer abler and more outspoken advocates than McKay. Not the least important of his actions was to ensure that in its formative period the GAA got valuable publicity in both the *Cork Examiner* and the *Cork Daily Herald*.

From a clue also found among Davin's papers one can now accurately identify the hitherto obscure Joseph O'Ryan, then apparently a stranger to Cusack, who described him as a solicitor of Thurles and Callan. Contemporary records in private ownership in his home town show him to have been a fellow athletics enthusiast of Davin from Carrick-on-Suir. From there he had presumably accompanied Davin to Thurles. From there, too, a year or so after his single connection with the GAA, he vanished mysteriously for good — or for ill, as seems more likely in those days when solicitors were rarely struck off their professional rolls.

None of the seven in Hayes's Hotel was as unrepresentative of those whose support Cusack was seeking as Thomas St George McCarthy, an RIC officer who had recently been appointed to the nearby town of Templemore. A Tipperary man whose father was a magistrate, McCarthy was a former student of Cusack, a former notable athlete and and (in 1882) a former Irish international rugby player.[3] Just what brought him back to Thurles can only be guessed at. He may have been invited by Cusack. He may have gone simply out of curiosity. He may have gone through genuine interest in athletics. He may have gone because his superiors felt he should keep an eye on the proceedings. Since he presumably did not come in uniform, one cannot dismiss the tradition in Thurles to this day that he just happened to be in town that day and met Davin or Cusack accidentally. Like O'Ryan, McCarthy never again went near the GAA, except as a spectator to Croke Park in the thirty years between his early retirement and his death only forty-seven years ago.

That the police authorities might have had more than a passing interest in the meeting is likely, since at least two of the seven GAA founders, Bracken and Power, were Fenians. Bracken, an impulsive egoist, would not at that stage of his life have been put off by the unexpected appearance of a police officer from the town where Bracken then had his home. But Frank Maloney of Nenagh might; hence his reluctance to attend the meeting itself, despite his known presence in Thurles that day.

Maloney was not the only local athletics enthusiast who apparently decided not to venture as far as the billiards-room of the hotel that November day in 1884. In the spurious list of twelve published in the inaccurate account of the historic meeting appear the names of T.K. Dwyer, Charles Culhane, M. Cantwell, William Delahunty and John Butler, all athletes from Thurles, and William Foley, another from Carrick-on-Suir. Perhaps they, too (like Maloney), felt they would not join a group that included a police officer of whose intentions they (unlike Cusack) would have been understandably suspicious.

None of this, however, explains the most striking thing about the foundation meeting of the GAA — why so few attended. Presumably Cusack had scattered his invitations far and wide — to athletic clubs all over the country, and to those supporters in

Kerry, Galway, Cork and probably elsewhere whom he had told of his plans. Indeed, some of the Cork athletes felt that he had overdone the canvassing before Thurles. Moreover, according to Cusack himself officers of the National League (the controlling body of the Home Rule party at constituency level) had also been circularised with the assistance of the League's national assistant secretary, Dan Hishon; he, it seems, had loaned Cusack his mailing-list.[4]

That Cusack fully appreciated the possible implications for the survival of his new body of the small attendance is suggested by his apparent attempt to exaggerate the extent of the promised support. Three weeks after Thurles the *Nation* newspaper published the text of eight of the sixty-odd letters of support Cusack had read at the meeting. It then transpired that at least one of the eight had come from one of those actually present at the meeting. The others were from Rev James Cantwell of Thurles, Michael Davitt, P.J. Maher of Clonmel, Joseph Johnson of Dundalk, A. Morrison Miller of the Caledonian Society, James Coll McLoughlin of Derry and John Hargrove of Clare — only one of whom (Johnson) was ever active in the GAA.

According to the *Cork Examiner* and *Cork Daily Herald* reports (for both of which McKay was presumably responsible), the meeting was 'poorly attended'. In addition, both Cork papers stated that because of the short notice several important clubs in the South did not send a representative. In marked contrast is Wyse Power's report in the *Leinster Leader*. According to this, the meeting was "well attended" — by, among others, 'a number of representatives of athletic clubs in Cork'.[5]

The short notice — only some five days, it seems — given of the meeting may go some distance to explain the smallness of the attendance. Yet one would have expected at least one of the Loughrea men (only seventy miles away), or somebody from Kerry (admittedly 100 miles distant) to have turned up. It seems curious, too, that none of his Dublin associates accompanied Cusack — not even J. J. Kenny of the Metropolitans, who is believed to have given a hand in the drafting of the carefully worded invitation.[6] There is a further mystery. Even if Cusack's name may have caused mixed feelings in some quarters, surely that of Davin on the invitation should have persuaded more than five people (excluding Davin and Cusack) to travel to Thurles?

In trying to account for the small attendance, one cannot avoid asking at this stage; why Thurles? After all, despite his disguised reference to that town as a likely venue in his August letter to Davin, Cusack had apparently maintained a personal preference for Cork well into October. His own explanation, that it was 'the most central (place) for the majority of the best athletes in Ireland', need not be taken seriously, although Thurles's location on the main Dublin-Cork railway line may have been a factor.[7] It is difficult to avoid the conclusion that the Tipperary town was selected largely out of deference to Davin, and perhaps also to a lesser extent because of the proximity of Croke, whose patronage Cusack had decided beforehand to seek, and to whom (according to local tradition) a message was sent during the course of the meeting.

As one moves on from Thurles to record the next activity of the GAA, one is confronted by still another complication that has never been explored, let alone answered. The second meeting of the new Association (a curious hybrid affair, as will shortly become apparent) took place in Cork city shortly after Christmas 1884, eight weeks later. Yet, apart from sporadic newspaper reports of the Thurles meeting (most of these apathetic or even hostile), one can find nothing to explain satisfactorily this long delay, and nothing to suggest what Cusack and his associates were up to during that period.

Given the speed, indeed the haste, with which he arranged the Thurles meeting, Cusack should have needed only a couple of weeks to arrange the Cork meeting. Since he actually took a couple of months, one is forced to speculate — to ask questions to which, after 100 years, one has no answer. Was there a doubt, or different opinions, about the wisdom of going ahead at all after Thurles? Did Cusack encounter difficulty in mustering further support from the Home Rule movement; or if, on the other hand, this was his idea, were some of his associates opposed to it? Was there, perhaps, opposition in Cork athletic circles, where Cusack's outrageous behaviour at the 1883 sports must still have rankled, to the holding of the vital meeting in that city?

The nature of the proceedings at the second meeting in Cork suggests a possible explanation of what Cusack and his associates were doing during that otherwise unexplained eight-week period. It was then, according to Cusack, that he sought the support of both Croke and Parnell for his new body. If, as seem almost certain, the presence in Thurles on 1 November of at least three Fenians (Bracken and Power in the hotel, with Maloney somewhere nearby) had come to the notice of Parnell, it would have been politically prudent of him to demand a price for any patronage he would give the new Association.

Such a demand if made — and the main decision taken in Cork prompts one to suggest that it was — it must have put Cusack in a difficult position. On the one hand, although he had been objecting to unionist domination of athletics for years, he had persuaded some Protestants (presumably unionist in outlook) to join his hurling crusade. They would in all probability have assumed that his crusade would be free of political connotations. On the other hand, having become resigned to the fact that his new body stood little chance of success without the support of public figures, he had successfully canvassed prominent members of Parnell's movement. In these circumstances he would have had little choice but to agree to any demand that may have been made by Parnell for a voice in the running of the new sports body set up by Cusack.

Another minor mystery connected with the Cork meeting, that may also partly explain the eight-week gap between Thurles and Cork, concerns a hurling match which, Cusack announced, would take place in Cork on the occasion of the second meeting. This suggests that he had expected that, together, the meeting and the game sponsored by the Association would make a major impact on the Cork sporting public. Somehow, however, his plans misfired; no hurling match materialised anywhere near Cork in the week of the GAA meeting in that city. According to another story, published twenty-seven years later, plans to hold an athletic meeting in conjunction with the Victoria Hotel meeting were thwarted by the garrison element in that city.[8]

2

On 11 December 1884, almost six weeks after the meeting in Hayes's Hotel, Cusack wrote to Parnell, Croke and Davitt, informing them of the decision to seek their patronage and formally seeking their agreement. All three replied inside ten days, and copies of their letters of acceptance were delivered by Cusack to the national and sporting organs in Dublin. At least three newspapers published the three letters in full, the *Freeman's Journal* on Christmas Eve and both *United Ireland* and the *Irishman* on 27 December.

Each letter, when compared to the other two, bears the stamp of the personality of its writer. That from Parnell, who was the first to reply, while warm in tone manages to retain an air of formality and is sparse in content. It runs to only four sentences — ninety-nine words in all. Agreeing with the objects of the GAA and expressing feelings of honour and appreciation, it ends by promising to work for the success of the new movement — giving Cusack what he wanted, no less, but certainly no more.

The letter from the founder of the Land League, while only about half as long again as Parnell's is altogether different in tone and content. Frank and to the point, Davitt's letter is enthusiastic about the new Association, while modestly professing to be conscious of how little its writer can do to further the GAA's aims. It is, above all, a letter from one fully sympathetic to the new Association to another with whom the writer is on friendly terms, and with whom the launching of the new movement has recently been fully discussed.

Quite different in every respect from those of his two co-patrons is the famous letter of Archbishop Croke agreeing to become a patron of the GAA. Running to over 700 words, this astonishing emotional outburst of patriotic sentiment has found a prominent place for a century in the official rule-book of the Association, which has understandably regarded it ever since as its charter. Politics, sport, culture, social customs, racial habits and rural life all find a place in this remarkable spontaneous piece of writing, which in places is far more racist in its sentiments than any of Cusack's writings of the previous ten years.

Frankly political in tone, Croke's letter expresses his dismay at the possible absorption of the traditional Irish way of life by the neighbouring island. He is particularly bitter about those Irish people who have adopted English customs — 'degenerate dandies' with 'masher habits' he called them in language curiously similar to that used frequently by Cusack from the mid-1870s onwards.

In a trenchant attack which first used a phrase later to be adopted by the GAA in one of its most controversial rules, he called tennis, polo, croquet and cricket 'foreign ... sports' which were alien to the Irish temperament. Again echoing a frequent theme of Cusack, he pointedly expressed the hope that nationalist organs of opinion would end their boycott of Irish sports. Finally, in a promise which he kept until his health gave way nearly twenty years later, he made it clear that he would 'be happy to do for [the GAA] all that I can'.

Ten days after Christmas Day of 1884, on the same day on which the patrons' letters appeared in the two nationalist weeklies, sixteen people attended in the Victoria Hotel in Cork what T.F. O'Sullivan accurately called 'a second meeting to promote the spread of the new organisation'. Both the composition and the proceedings of this gathering were in some important respects even more curious than those of the Thurles meeting. As at Hayes's Hotel, the principal decision taken in Cork was to have a lasting impact on Irish sport — as well as on the Association that had been founded in Thurles eight weeks earlier.

Of those present at the Victoria Hotel only half are identifiable a century later as genuine athletics enthusiasts — Davin, Cusack, McKay, Bracken, and Messrs A. O'Driscoll, W.J.M. Barry and J.E. Kennedy of the Cork Athletic Club, to which McKay also belonged. Of five others — J.T. O'Regan, John King, Dr Riordan, J. O'Callaghan and W. Cotter, it seems likely that they attended as prominent local Home Rule personalities.

The two surviving accounts of this meeting — from O'Sullivan and McKay — differ in details. However, they agree on one thing: politicians and politics dominated it. Alderman Paul Madden, Lord Mayor-elect of Cork, presided rather than Davin, and the main business was piloted through by John O'Connor (soon to be foisted by Parnell on an unwilling Tipperary party machine as Home Rule MP) and Daniel Horgan, councillor of Cork Corporation and later first chairman of the Cork county board of the GAA.

On O'Connor's proposal, with Horgan seconding, it was decided that the Central Committee of the GAA ('elected to carry out the work of the Association') would consist of the officers (Davin, Cusack, McKay and Power), the Organising Committee of the National League (numbering twenty-five) and — almost as an afterthought — two delegates from every recognised athletic club in Ireland. According to McKay, Cusack then informed the meeting that the League's executive had given its adherence to the GAA, an understatement if ever there was one.

The remainder of the business transacted almost suggests a second meeting, perhaps held after the departure of the Cork Home Rule caucus. Cusack assured the meeting that with the selection of the three patrons the new body was now firmly established and guaranteed success. He announced also that he had secured a weekly column of space for GAA events in *United Ireland*, and read a letter from a brother of Davin challenging any county to meet a team of footballers from Tipperary. Finally, since the decision made at Thurles to draft rules had obviously not been acted on, an identical decision was now made in Cork.

This meeting, at which GAA members were almost certainly in a minority, was to have far-reaching implications for the Association in both the short and the long terms. Because it appeared to make the GAA an ally of the constitutional nationalist movement — even to make it dependent for its existence on the support of that movement — it was bound at least to alienate supporters of national pastimes who were not nationalists. Some belonging to this class had been among Cusack's associates since 1883. Moreover, by sheltering under the umbrella of the National League, Cusack and Davin had made it difficult to refute the allegation — which Cusack's enemies lost little time in making — that his decision to found the GAA was politically motivated, and that the Association was merely a new wing of the nationalist movement.

That Cusack's opponents in the athletics world would oppose his new body once they saw it appearing to succeed goes without saying. However, by lining up so openly with the Home Rule organisation he gave his critics unexpectedly useful ammunition to use against him. In addition, the proceedings in Cork ensured that the attack on the GAA came sooner rather than later. It also led to a more determined campaign against the Association, because it could now be claimed by Cusack's opponents to be merely a subsidiary of the National League.

On the nationalist movement itself, the Victoria Hotel meeting was also bound to have an impact. By taking the new sports organisation so speedily and so openly under its wing, the Home Rule leaders were giving notice to other sections of the nationalist movement that any intrusion by them into the GAA would not be welcome. There can be little doubt that Parnell was anxious to keep to a minimum Fenian influence in the new Association, already seen to have begun with the presence in Thurles on 1 November of Bracken, Power and Maloney.

By far the most important result of the Cork meeting, however, and perhaps the major long-term impact on Irish sport of the GAA, was the unequivocal and exclusive identification from the start of the Association with the nationalist movement. This, in turn, produced two effects. It led to the GAA, at a vital stage in nationalist affairs early this century, playing a significant role in the growth and ultimate major successes of the nationalist movement, particularly in the ten years from 1913 to 1922. It also made of the GAA a kind of training college, where articulate and ambitious young nationalists served their political apprenticeship before starting a public career in one or other of the purely political nationalist organisations.

Whether, indeed, such a marriage of nationalist politics and national games so close as that begun in the Victoria Hotel was something that Michael Cusack ever seriously planned is open to doubt. There is evidence that it was the turn of the century before he was converted to the inevitability of the idea and saw its advantages to each partner to this union. However, whether he had in mind in the 1880s such a marriage is one of the yet unanswered (and probably now unanswerable) questions about the founder of the GAA. It suffices, perhaps, at this stage to indicate that there is evidence to suggest that what Cusack had envisaged at some time before November 1884 was a sports body that would cross both political and religious lines. His model was the Irish language movement from the mid-1870s, particularly the Gaelic Union from the time he had become active in it.

What actually happened to the Association Cusack founded was, of course, something quite different. It was also to prove somewhat different from what one suspects Parnell and his lieutenants in the Irish Party had in mind. Before the 1886 athletics season had ended, Cusack, in a public disagreement with the secretary of the National League (Tim Harrington MP) was to succeed in decisively breaking the close links that had developed between the GAA and the League and Party. In doing so he deprived his enemies in the unionist athletic camp, who by then were engaged in a concerted campaign aimed at annihilating the GAA, of their strongest argument for opposing him.

3

Before his opponents commenced hostilities against the GAA, indeed while they were gathering their forces for the opening skirmish, Cusack, Davin and McKay began the important work of building on the foundations laid in Thurles and Cork. On 17 January 1885, just three weeks after the Cork meeting, the first important meeting of the GAA took place in Hayes's Hotel, Thurles. This switch back to the venue of the foundation meeting marked the abandonment of Cork as the headquarters in favour of

Thurles, although no formal decision to that effect was made.

However, both the attendance at this second Thurles meeting and some of its decisions show that the Cork influence on the infant Association was not only being maintained but even increased. Ten people attended — four of the seven founders (Davin, Cusack, McKay and Bracken), as well as Maloney and John Fahy of the Nenagh Cricket Club, and two delegates (Ryan and Dunne) of the North Tipperary Hurling Club. Missing were Power (who was to remain missing for all of 1885 and some of 1886), O'Ryan and McCarthy, the last two never to return.

The first of four decisions was less formal than it may sound. Five vice-presidents were appointed, of whom three were from Cork — J. E. Kennedy of the Cork AC, J. F. Murphy, a Cork city football enthusiast, and W. J. M. Barry, a notable athlete with Queen's College, Cork. Appointed the GAA's first handicapper was Cusack's antagonist of 1883, J. F. O'Crowley of Cork, who thus secured what was the most important post in the athletics sphere in the new body. The other two vice-presidents were Bracken and J. H. Stewart, the latter a forgotten athletics figure from Tyrone then resident in Dublin, a Protestant who had supported Cusack's reforms from at least 1882.

The next decision was to make any athlete who had participated in a non-GAA meeting ineligible for GAA athletics meetings held after 17 March, 1885. Although destined to be a major source of controversy for the following year, this ruling was not in any sense the start of the famous GAA 'ban' that lasted until 1971. So far as Cusack was concerned, he was now merely retaliating against his opponents with a similar boycott to that which they had been operating for some time in attempting to force Irish athletes to come in under the umbrella of the AAA. Whether this new GAA rule was wise is quite another question.

The Thurles meeting also adopted rules for hurling, football and the principal athletic events; those for running, walking and cycling closely followed the AAA rules. Finally, the principle of one club for each parish, to which the GAA still strives to adhere over a century later, was also agreed on.

The effect on Cusack's opponents of the decision taken at the second Thurles meeting was immediate and two-fold. Whatever doubts they may have had about the permanency of the GAA because of the eight-week silence between the first two meetings, it was now clear to them that the new Association, with the blessing of its three influential patrons, was here to stay. Secondly, it was equally clear to them that in areas coming under GAA control the jurisdiction of the AAA would face a serious challenge from mid-March 1885. Concerted action to stop the GAA in its tracks was now called for.

The preliminary skirmish in what was to be a bitter struggle between the GAA and its opponents was not long in coming. On 22 January, only five days after the second Thurles meeting, a meeting in Dublin of the Irish Cyclists' Association suspended its ordinary business 'to discuss ... the Gaelic Athletic Association'. The main object of the ensuing discussion was manifestly to canvass support for a bigger and broader-based meeting of athletes fixed for two days later. At this, war would be formally declared on Cusack and his associates.

Although itself unimportant and unrepresentative, the ICA meeting, which was attended by only thirteen delegates from five Dublin cycling clubs, anticipated some of the intemperate attacks that lay ahead for the GAA. One speaker called on athletes 'to unite ... to quash the Gaelic Union', an unfortunate (and inaccurate) phrase that was to be repeatedly thrown back by Cusack and provoke an immediate and acid comment from the *Freeman's Journal*, that 'if the bicyclists ... imagine they are going to quash (Croke, Parnell and Davitt) they are very much mistaken'. Other ICA speakers contented themselves with offensive personal remarks about Cusack and O'Crowley.

Two days later, on 24 January, in response to a circular signed by J. G. Beatty, J.H. Christian and J. Berry (all from Dublin harrier clubs), forty-one delegates from eighteen athletic clubs (all but four of them from Dublin, and six of them merely cycling clubs) met in the Wicklow Hotel. Since the ICA meeting had been private, this was the first public opposition to the GAA. Exclusively unionist in political complexion, it was sufficiently united to lead to a further meeting a month later, from which a rival organisation to the GAA was to emerge.

This first Wicklow Hotel meeting — there was to be a second — adopted three resolutions. These, together with the views expressed by the leading speakers, give an idea of the line of attack that was to be directed against the GAA for most of the following year. First, the right of the new Association ('a self-constituted body ... formed on political lines') to make laws for Irish athletes was repudiated. Secondly, it was decided to ask each athletic club to attend a meeting to form a new amateur athletic association. Finally, the meeting assured the GAA of its willingness to assist them in reviving Irish games — so long, of course, as they kept out of athletics and confined their activities to hurling and Irish football.

Four weeks later again, on 21 February 1885, came the formal establishment of the Irish Amateur Athletic Association at a second meeting in the Wicklow Hotel, held under the auspices of an *ad hoc* group called the Irish Amateur Athletic Club. This time also forty-one delegates representing twenty clubs (again mostly from Dublin) or bodies attended. So did Cusack, at the request of Davin, who had notified the organisers in advance of his request. From Cusack, ably assisted by McKay and O'Crowley (both of whom represented the Cork AC), the GAA's case against the proposal to form a rival body was put to the meeting. However, the mood of the delegates proved to be almost entirely against the GAA speakers.

From the start of this meeting Cusack cannot have been in any doubt about the hostility of the overwhelming majority, many of whom knew him (perhaps too well) for up to ten years. Despite the conciliatory tone of Davin's letter, a long wrangle developed about Cusack's right to remain. Eventually he was allowed to stay, but only in his capacity as a journalist from *United Ireland* — a ruling which, after a characteristically abusive attack by him on the organisers of the meeting, silenced Cusack.

At an early stage both McKay and O'Crowley argued convincingly against the need for a second athletics body. McKay denied that the GAA was a politically inspired body, and assured the meeting that it had room for all athletes. O'Crowley, after making the case for Home Rule in Irish athletics, expanded on a point McKay had mentioned. Earlier attempts to found a body like the IAAA had failed and were now only being revived as a way of crushing the GAA, which (unlike the IAAA) would not be Dublin-dominated in its outlook. While dissociating himself from Cusack's tactics, he accused his opponents of being motivated by personal antipathy to Cusack.

That the organisers of the meeting (who would have kept details of it secret, had not McKay insisted on publicity) were determined to form their rival body is clear from the absence of any attempt to answer the Cork delegates' arguments.[9] J.A.H. Christian, who chaired both Wicklow Hotel meetings, declared the resolution to form the IAAA passed unanimously, although several clubs (Monasterevin, the Caledonians and the Freeman's Journal among them) had declared their neutrality. At least three others (two from Ulster and Queen's College, Cork) declined to commit themselves. The two Corkmen (McKay and O'Crowley), were naturally opposed to the 'unanimous' decision.

Although destined to last for almost forty years until the GAA gave up control of athletics in 1922, the IAAA had almost as shaky a start as the GAA three months earlier. Apart from those which withheld support initially, some of the Ulster athletes were obviously fearful of control from Dublin. Moreover, several of the clubs that attended this first meeting of the IAAA later changed over to the GAA — those of Cork, Limerick, the Freeman's Journal, Tullamore and Clane among them. Furthermore, it is ironic to observe that, if one disregards the delegates from clubs opposed to the IAAA's formation, this body was effectively founded by twenty delegates from ten Dublin clubs, of which seven were for harriers only and one for cyclists only. Yet for most of 1885 this Association continued to assert that the GAA was an unrepresentative self-constituted body!

Cusack's opponents, henceforth the IAAA, may have silenced him at the Wicklow Hotel. But they were powerless to prevent him from making full use of the columns of the two main nationalist papers. From the first issue in 1885 of *United Ireland* he directed a withering fire into the ranks of his enemies — until some eighteen months later his own colleagues, some of them wounded by his increasingly wild shots, decided that their Secretary was doing his Association more harm than good.

The editorial 'Irish Athletics' in *United Ireland* of 3 January 1885 (whose authorship Cusack later admitted in court) was both a restrained statement of the case for a body like the GAA and a blunt warning that 'the freezing neglect of the Press' of national games was at an end. Four weeks later, on 31 January, came the first of Cusack's own column 'National Pastimes', which was to continue under his control until the middle of 1886. In this opening article Cusack strenuously denied that the GAA had political objectives, and contradicted his opponents' allegation that his initial aim had been to encourage hurling to the exclusion of athletics — a line of attack they persisted in for many more months, until it became clear that the GAA had no intention of leaving athletics to the IAAA.

A month later, on 28 February, Cusack was at his most effective in a scathing and witty analysis of the Wicklow Hotel proceedings of the previous Saturday. Four weeks later again on 21 March, he wound up his opening counter-attack on his opponents by being as explicit on their politics as they had been on the GAA's. The Dublin athletic clubs, he pointed out, were run by 'extreme Conservatives', who (if they joined the GAA) could surely hold their own against the occasional Nationalist MP who might attend a GAA executive meeting. All that his Association hoped to do was to restore the balance of power after the long period during which Irish athletics had been in non- or anti-nationalist hands.

More or less contemporaneously with his column in *United Ireland,* which he mainly devoted to news of the growth of the GAA, Cusack also used the correspondence columns of the *Freeman's Journal* when an opportunity arose. It did so three times in the first three months of 1885. In these letters he not merely came to the support of Davin, but at the same time scored two victories over his most articular opponent, J.A.H. Christian, now assistant secretary of the IAAA.

On 13 February, Davin, in a long letter, dealt with many aspects of the athletics controversy. Trenchantly making the case for the existence of the GAA, he denied any intention of controlling cycling or harrying. He pointed out the anomaly of an English body (the AAA) making rules to bind Irish athletes. He called for support for Irish football in preference to rugby, which he claimed was unsuited to the Irish temperament. He suggested, too, that the GAA would not 'be so easily quashed as some people think'.

The following day, in a letter so full of errors that it took Cusack only another forty-eight hours to silence him, Christian rushed into print to reply to Davin. Proving that Christian had misquoted Croke, Cusack went on to rebut Christian's argument that Davin and O'Crowley were the only reputable athletes at the first Thurles meeting. Four weeks later, when Christian returned to the attack in reply to a second letter by Cusack, the latter again exposed Christian in another apparently deliberate misquotation, this time of the terms of the invitation to the foundation meeting of the GAA.

The bitterness of these attacks on Cusack by IAAA spokesmen and the *Irish Sportsman* showed that they recognised him as the real founder of the GAA. He was accused of the most improper motives, personal and political, in starting the Association; it was even suggested that the GAA was to be a way of advertising his Academy, which was said to be in dire financial straits. In stark contrast, the IAAA deferred to Davin, even going to the length of withdrawing a motion critical of him at the second Wicklow Hotel meeting. Their attitude to the popular Tipperary athlete proved how prestigious a figure he was to lead the new association.

Eventually, perhaps goaded by his taunts and by the early successes of the GAA, Cusack's opponents overplayed their hands. Rejecting a half-hearted apology for a satirical but scurrilous poem (which parodied a popular Gilbert and Sullivan song) published by the *Irish Sportsman,* Cusack sued the paper's owner, Mrs. Mary Dunbar, for libel. The full day's hearing before a jury in the High Court in June 1885 ended in success for Cusack after evidence which, when sifted a century later, yields some nuggets of information about the founder of the GAA.

Footnotes
1. *Chicago Citizen,* 22.9.1888.
2. *FJ,* 7.1.1905; *Irish Freedom,* February 1911.
3. PRO, RIC files, MFA 24/16.
4. *Irish Weekly Independent,* Christmas No., 1902; *Chicago Citizen,* 22.9.1888.
5. *Leinster Leader,* 8.11.1884.
6. *An Poblacht,* 9.4.1932.
7. *Shamrock,* 25.10.1884.
8. 'Celt' in *Irish Freedom,* Feb. 1911.
9. *Irish Weekly Independent,* Christmas No., 1902.

Principal Sources
Cork Examiner, 1884 and 1885
Freeman's Journal, 1884 and 1885
Irishman, 1884 and 1885
Irish Sportsman, 1884 and 1885
Nation, 1884 and 1885
O'Sullivan, T.F., *Story of the GAA* (Dublin, 1916)
Sport, 1884 and 1885
United Ireland, 1884 and 1885

CHAPTER SEVEN

THE FOUNDER IS DISMISSED

1885–1886

The success of the GAA in its first year was phenomenal. Except in Dublin, the campaign of its opponents to kill off the Association, which was led by the IAAA, had practically no effect. So fast did the GAA grow in 1885 that Cusack justifiably later claimed that 'it spread like a prairie fire'. Even before its enemies had gathered their forces in February 1885, the Association had begun to spread all over the south and east of the country. This growth continued unchecked all through the spring, naturally reaching its climax during the summer athletics season. It lasted well into the late autumn; by then, the IAAA, by publicly seeking terms for a peaceful co-existence between the two bodies, had effectively acknowledged defeat.

In the Dublin area, on the other hand, the GAA's growth was sporadic until well into 1886. For several reasons there was opposition to the Association in the city. Despite the success of the Metropolitan Club, hurling was almost unknown there, and the existence on an organised basis of both rugby and soccer militated against the spread of Irish football. So determined was opposition to Cusack in Dublin athletic circles that until mid-1886 he was denied a ground to stage a meeting there.[1] Yet almost from the start, in some of the many villages then scattered around the city, GAA clubs did spring up — in Ringsend, Blackrock, Dalkey, Glasthule, Drumcondra and Dun Laoire. When, largely through the efforts of Wyse Power, an organised campaign was begun which culminated in the establishment towards the end of 1886 of the Dublin county board, these clubs formed the nucleus of what quickly became one of the most powerful units in the GAA. By 1887 also, several playing-grounds had become available in or near the city.

Elsewhere — in cities, towns, villages and rural parishes all over Munster and Leinster — athletics meetings were organised and hurling and football matches arranged week-end after week-end for the eight months of March to October 1885, all under GAA auspices. In nearly every case, these spontaneous gatherings and contests were either preceded or followed by the formation of a new GAA club. The traditional athletic contests of the cross-roads and fair-greens predominated at these meetings, many of which also witnessed, for the first time in nearly half a century, hurling or football games or both. Handball and bowls were also revived in areas where they had nearly died out in the years after the famines of the 1840s.

Between these hundreds of sports meetings and those that had been held in the provinces since the revival of athletics in the 1860s there was an important difference. Because the new association founded in Thurles had the blessing of the three leaders of the nationalist community, most of the meetings from 1885 onwards were controlled by genuine representatives of that community. Gone for ever was the patronage of the local landlord or titled member of the landed gentry. Instead, management of athletics passed in most parts of Munster and Leinster (and, soon after 1886, in Connacht, too) into the hands of local nationalists, often officers of the National League or members of the Catholic clergy. At the same time the two games of hurling and Irish football (soon to be called 'Gaelic' after the new body) began to be revived on a countrywide basis through the playing of inter-club and inter-parish games, often in association with local athletic meetings.

Probably nobody more vividly summarised the effect of this astonishing nationwide activity in the first year of the GAA than its first historian, T. F. O'Sullivan, who himself grew up in an area where, and at a time when, memories of that period were still fresh, and who was also involved in the GAA from his teens. 'Hurling gained a new lease of life. Football was revived. Running, jumping, weight-throwing, wrestling, bowling and handball were practised in districts where they had become only a tradition ... Thousands of people eagerly gathered to witness hurling and football matches and athletic contests, and the dull monotony of Irish rural life was dispelled for ever. A new spirit had been created in the country.'

A complete account of this second revival of athletics in the provinces is outside the scope of this study of the man who was mainly, if not solely, responsible for it. In any event, largely because (through lack of press coverage) many of the smaller sports meetings of 1885 were never recorded, such a record would be almost impossible to compile. In many cases, it is the known existence of an organised GAA club before the end of that year, or oral tradition handed down by families still involved in the Association a century later, that alone makes it virtually certain that the first meeting or match, which was invariably associated with the foundation of the club, had actually taken place.

The first sports meeting known to have been held under GAA auspices took place near Macroom in Co. Cork two weeks after the foundation of the Association. Exceptionally in this case, it does not appear that any club grew out of the event, for the first recognised GAA club was that formed in Clara in Co. Offaly in mid-December 1884 — itself, contrariwise, not apparently the result of any local sports meeting. Then on 6 January 1885, two Galway clubs (Killimor and Ballinakill) played the first hurling game under GAA rules before 6,000 people, Killimor winning. Six weeks later in mid-February, Kilkenny and Callan failed to score in the first football match under GAA rules.

By the end of April, with the Association only six months old, it had spread to six more counties — Dublin, Clare, Tipperary, Derry, Kildare and Antrim. Early in January, a sports meeting was held at Tulla in Clare; in February, a hurling club was formed at Clonard in Belfast and a hurling game between the Metropolitans and Cusack's Academy was played. Four clubs (Nenagh, Ballyneale, Silvermines and Clonmel) appeared in Tipperary in March and one in Derry (near Magherafelt). March 1885 also saw the affiliation of two new athletic clubs from Kildare — Clane and Straffan. April saw several more new Cork and Tipperary clubs join, among those in Cork being the pre-1884 Cork AC, to which McKay and O'Crowley belonged. Football played under GAA rules was reported that same month in both Cork and Kildare.

With the start of summer 1885 the rate of growth began to increase rapidly. In May, clubs in at least six new counties affiliated to the Association — Cavan, Westmeath, Mayo, Wicklow, Louth and Down. June brought the earliest report of GAA activity in Wexford and Kerry, the latter county also figuring in the list of sports held in July and August. Limerick was first mentioned in GAA reports in July and Waterford in August. In the five months from June to September, GAA sports meetings, which often included hurling or football matches, were held in no less than eleven counties of Munster and Leinster, with Roscommon's earliest sports meetings under GAA rules being held in October.

On 4 July, the same day on which the *Irish Sportsman* (now the mouthpiece of his opponents) described the GAA as 'semi-defunct', Cusack in *United Ireland* claimed that the GAA was firmly established in Munster and Leinster. The frequent reports throughout 1885 in the *Freeman's Journal,* now at last giving the Association's activities at least sporadic coverage, support Cusack's view. By the end of the year, the GAA was well organised in all six Munster counties and in at least seven Leinster counties — Dublin, Louth, Kildare, Kilkenny, Offaly, Westmeath and Wexford. Clubs had also affiliated from three counties in Connacht — Galway, Mayo and Roscommon, and from another four in Ulster — Derry, Down, Antrim and Cavan. Little more than a year after its foundation the GAA was now actively involved in athletics, hurling and football in twenty counties out of the thirty-two.

For this remarkable and immediate success of the GAA in its first year almost all of the credit must go to Cusack. No matter how important Davin's support was, no matter how prestigious the patronage of Croke, Parnell and Davitt, the idea of the Association was Cusack's alone. Without his planning, his successful canvassing of support, and above all his equally successful appeal to the provinces, the GAA would never have got beyond the drawing-board stage — where several similar projects had failed in the previous few years, including one in 1877 that had got the support of both Davin and Nally. Moreover, by concentrating almost exclusively on athletics in the GAA's first year, Cusack achieved two other important objectives. He defeated his opponents in their own sphere of activity, and he made it much easier for the GAA to concentrate on hurling and football from 1886 onwards when it had been built on a solid basis over the greater part of the country.

Curiously, and contrary to popular belief, Cusack himself attended surprisingly few of these hundreds of GAA events in 1885. Indeed, the founder of the GAA seems to have turned up at only four provincial venues that year. Of course, two — Tralee in mid-June and Tramore in early October — were of such importance that he could not have missed them. The other two he managed to squeeze into one week-end at the end of May, when after a trip to Drogheda to establish the first branch of the Association in Lough, Cusack travelled to Kells in Meath on his way home.[2]

By comparison, McKay and O'Crowley (but not, it seems, Davin or Power) travelled much more widely than Cusack in 1885. In fairness to him, it has to be pointed out that none of the other four had a private school to run on a full-time basis, and that two (McKay and Power) were journalists whose work enabled them to travel extensively from home. Moreover, none of the four was obliged to fill a weekly column as Cusack was in *United Ireland,* nor did any of them devote so much time as he did in writing letters to the newspapers in furtherance of the GAA's aims. However, the substance of the serious complaints made in 1886 about his regime as principal secretary make one wonder if Cusack's almost complete absence from provincial meetings in 1885 may have been a factor in the groundswell of criticism that built up against him soon after the GAA was a year old.

On the other hand, Cusack missed none of the three important indoor meetings of the GAA in 1886. As already recorded, he attended the meeting in Thurles in mid-January at which the rules were adopted. He was also present in Thurles for the meeting in mid-July at which the break with the National League after the Tralee sports of mid-June (shortly to be explained) was formalised. Finally, he took a prominent part in the Association's first annual convention (in Thurles again), held at the end of October and continued four months later in February 1886.

Most important of all, Cusack was at the GAA's Tralee sports on 17 June 1886, an event which was a turning-point in the Association's relations both with the Irish Party and its umbrella body, the National League. Indeed, his masterly handling of this crucial episode can be seen in retrospect to have marked the climax of Cusack's regime as secretary of the GAA. It went far to repair the damage caused by the hybrid Victoria Hotel meeting in Cork the previous Christmas, which (as already pointed out) had been dominated by politicians.

Tralee, in effect, became the venue for the first (and in many respects the last) open outdoor confrontation between the GAA and the IAAA. The County Kerry Athletic & Cricket Club, one of the few IAAA clubs in Munster, had fixed its annual sports for 17 June in Tralee, whereupon the local branch of the GAA decided to hold its sports on the same day in the same town. When the local Irish Party MP, Edward Harrington (brother of Tim Harrington MP, a friend of Cusack) publicly gave his support to the IAAA, Cusack came down specially from Dublin some days beforehand to organise the GAA's rival event. On his arrival he secured the support of a popular local priest, Fr Matt McMahon of Kilmeen, to counter the loss of the influential Harrington.

On the day of the rival sports meetings there was no doubt about which association won. Some 10,000 spectators attended the GAA event to watch about 500 competitors; nearby, the cream of IAAA clubs from all over the country competed to an almost empty stadium.[3] If, as one suspects, Harrington opposed the GAA locally because it was controlled by two Fenians (Moore Stack and Maurice Moynihan, a future secretary of the GAA), the result of his action must have dismayed him. Inside a week the local INL branch had dismissed him from its presidency, and the same day it fell to his brother Tim in his capacity as national secretary of the INL publicly to sever all formal links between the League and the GAA.

The GAA's triumph at Tralee, of which Cusack was the main architect, had four important results. It demonstrated, both to its own followers and to its opponents, how successful the Association had become only seven months after its foundation. It prevented the spread of the IAAA in Munster, which from then had gradually to take second place to the GAA in athletics in Munster. It taught the GAA a valuable lesson it has never forgotten in the following hundred or so years — that in the Catholic clergy it had (and still has) a powerful source of support which no other Irish sports body has managed to tap so extensively.

Above all, the Tralee episode became the occasion — indeed, one suspects the excuse for — the end of the uneasy alliance between the National League and the GAA that had been so hastily begun in Cork six months before. One suspects, too, that Cusack gained much more from this link than did Parnell, some of whose local officers in several counties got caught up in personal rivalries over posts in the GAA. On 24 June the secretary of the League, Tim Harrington MP, wrote on behalf of the Organising Committee (which had been co-opted *en masse* on to the GAA executive at Cork) to the Tralee branch, dissolving it and stating that the League had no connection with the GAA, insisting that any promotion of the GAA by any member of the INL had been unauthorised.

A month later, the GAA, which had capitalised widely on the support of INL branches and officers all over the country, responded in moderate language to the League's disclaimer. The executive of the Association, meeting in Thurles on 18 July, declared that it needed no support from any other body and had no intention of damaging 'any existing Irish national organisation'. This was not, however, by any means the end of co-operation between the two bodies, which continued right up to the 1916 Rising. But it made easier further infiltration of the GAA by the Fenians — one of whom, Bracken, had proposed the executive's 18 July declaration:

The Tralee sports was not Cusack's only victory in June 1885. Some two weeks earlier a libel action which he brought against the Dunbars, for having published in their *Irish Sportsman* in January a poem insulting and belittling him, had been heard before a jury in the High Court in Dublin. After a day's hearing, Cusack was awarded £10 damage and his costs. Considering that he had claimed £500 this may seem to have been a Pyrrhic victory; yet to have won at all in the circumstances was remarkable. A century later, the case is principally of interest for the portraits it provides of the principal personalities involved, Cusack and John Dunbar.

The defamation was contained in a 32-line, four-verse parody of a popular sketch in the Gilbert and Sullivan opera *Patience*. In case any reader of the paper might overlook the point, a brief explanatory introduction referred to 'the Central Secretary of the GAA'. Moreover, the poem was attributed to 'Bryan Merryboy, a junior poet of Clare', an obvious jibe at Cusack's well-known facility for reciting in full the famous eighteenth-century 1,100-line poem *The Midnight Court* by the Clare teacher Brian Merriman.

As usual in such parodies the desired effect — to ridicule its subject — was achieved mostly by exaggerating his personal traits, something James Joyce was to do to an older Cusack many years later. However, in addition (as the preface explained also) skilful use was made throughout of phrases frequently used by Cusack in conversation. Again, lest their significance might be lost on the unwary reader, these were either enclosed in quotation-marks or printed in italics.

Before the court hearing an attempt had been made by the Dunbars to settle the action. These negotiations broke down, however, because the defendant (Dunbar's mother, proprietress of the paper) was not prepared to donate a sum to the Gaelic Union in settlement of the claim. Instead, a small monetary lodgement was made in court, and this was added to the sum awarded to Cusack when a verdict in his favour was reached by the jury.

In court Cusack was represented by Denis Sullivan, brother of the late A. M. Sullivan MP of the *Nation*, and by the later famous Tim Healy MP, then a confidant of Parnell. The reading to the jury of the parody caused much amusement, and enabled the defendants to create the impression that Cusack was taking far too seriously something merely intended in jest. However, Cusack's performance in the witness-box, especially under cross-examination, when he combined frankness, honesty and humour, was masterly.

He also showed shrewdness in emphasising his Academy's successes in RIC examinations, saying that the offensive tone of the poem was, if taken seriously, calculated to injure him professionally. Indeed, so shaken were his opponents that they almost lost the case on a technicality which the judge brought to their notice.

That Cusack impressed the jury is evident from the verdict in his favour. He also won the sympathy of the bench. Mr. Justice Harrison cut short an attempt to sneer at Archbishop Croke, and the emphasis in his charge to the jury leaned discreetly towards the plaintiff. Small as the award was, the result represented a significant victory for Cusack, and it must also have been a worthwhile free advertisement for his Academy.

The publicity the case received in all sections of the press cannot have done the GAA any harm either; quite the opposite is likely to have been the impact on fair-minded readers. At a time when the Association had just established itself permanently on the Irish sporting scene, its opponents were shown up in a court of law as shabby and small-minded, some of them (like Dunbar) hurt by the loss of income which the rise of the GAA had caused them. So bitter had Dunbar and his circle become against Cusack that they had circulated this poem, picked up at a private smoking concert, without a thought of the consequences, for inside a week the *Irish Sportsman* has published a half-hearted apology which Cusack had rejected as inadequate.

In retrospect, however, it has to be admitted that, even when stripped of its elements of caricature, the portrait of Cusack revealed by the libellous poem is far from flattering. One gets an impression that he had, if anything, become more abrasive in recent years — boorish in speech, garish in garb, generally eccentric in his whole manner. How he hoped his nationalist philosophy would ever win support from the elitist urban circle he continued to preach raucously at is beyond comprehension, for qualities such as tact and discretion were obviously totally foreign to his nature. It is not surprising that, when (all too soon) he came to treat his own colleagues just as viciously as he had his opponents, they did not tolerate such behaviour for long.

2

Even before the 1885 athletics season had ended, the war between the GAA and the IAAA had erupted again. The resumption of hostilities was marked by a decision of the IAAA in mid-August to impose its own ban on GAA athletes from 1 September, in retaliation for the GAA's ban from the previous 17 March. The IAAA ban was supplemented by one imposed by the Irish Cyclists Association, which had supported the IAAA in its campaign against the GAA from the start — indeed, even before the IAAA had been founded, as has already been explained. These two rival bans were to dominate the activities of the two rival associations for the next six months.

By the autumn of 1885, however, the tactical advantage had swung clearly in favour of the GAA. Several factors accounted for this. Its spectacular growth during the summer contrasted with the stagnation of the IAAA, which over the whole country could only muster thirty clubs, most of them in the Dublin area. For publicity purposes the IAAA had nothing to match Cusack's weekly column in *United Ireland*, the appearance in November 1885 (when the war was nearly over) of a weekly IAAA organ only somehow serving to emphasise the cultural and political gulfs between the two bodies.[4] Moreover, Cusack's victory in the High Court, about which he presumably boasted far and wide, cannot have helped the image of his opponents.

Above all, the independent stance the GAA had taken against the Home Rule movement over the rival sports meetings in Tralee had done much to remove the main argument of the IAAA — that its rival was a mere political appendage of the nationalist movement. At the GAA executive meeting in Thurles in mid-July the Association had followed up its victory at Tralee with a formal declaration that 'although a thoroughly national one' the GAA was 'not a political association', and that its platform was 'sufficiently wide for all classes and creeds'. While welcoming assistance from every quarter (the resolution continued), it was not asking for and did not need support from any other body. This independent stance was evidenced by the continued participation in Cusack's club of hurlers (former hurley-players) of unionist outlook and by the presence in the GAA at administrative level of Protestants like J.H. Stewart of Tyrone and William Fisher of Waterford.

The IAAA ban produced no public reaction from either Cusack or any other officer of the GAA. For most of September they were all probably too busy planning for the GAA's first annual national athletic championships in October. Originally planned for August, it had been postponed because of the Association's failure to get suitable grounds in Dublin. Eventually the venue was changed to Tramore, one of the few provincial grounds with covered stand accommodation. There the event was successfully held on 6 October, the last major outdoor event of the GAA's first year.

Three weeks later Archbishop Croke made his first major intervention in GAA affairs since becoming its principal patron ten months earlier. The first annual convention (now known as its congress) of the GAA was fixed for Thurles on 31 October, and it was obvious that the question of the rival bans would be debated there. The day before the convention opened, the *Freeman's Journal*, in a carefully-worded editorial, called for an end to the two boycotts of the rival athletic bodies. Although critical of the IAAA's reluctance to permit traditional Irish events, it urged both bodies to open each other's meetings to all athletes. Within twenty-four hours there was an angry reaction from Cusack, who understandably drew the paper's attention to the conciliatory tone of his executive's resolution of mid-July. In response, however, the *Freeman* suggested that the first move in ending the boycotts should come from the GAA.

As if stung by the tone of Cusack's letter, the *Freeman* in its next issue was obliged to reveal the source of its original plea. A letter from Croke to the GAA, suggesting the revocation of what he called its 'exclusion rule' was published, and the paper urged both bodies to accept the archbishop's proposal. Meanwhile the first session of the GAA convention had been held, but discussion of Croke's letter took place behind closed doors and a decision was deferred to the adjourned meeting fixed for 27 February 1886 — to allow, it later transpired, for a consensus to be reached within the GAA itself in the intervening four months. However, in a short letter to the *Freeman* on 5 November (clearly authorised by his executive), Cusack indicated that Croke's suggestion would be accepted and that the GAA ban on IAAA athletes would be lifted at the next meeting.

Against this conciliatory background a movement now began to grow inside the IAAA for a merger with the GAA, prompted perhaps by a curious but lone plea made at the Thurles convention by Wyse Power for some form of mutual pact between the two bodies. However, inside the IAAA, it soon transpired, there were also conflicting opinions. As so often happens in such cases, each side had its own group of die-hards. Nevertheless, both associations were to continue to share control of Irish athletics — sometimes in mutual distrust, sometimes in limited harmony — for another thirty-six years, until the establishment of a new Irish State in 1922 radically altered the athletic scene.

The proposal for a merger with the GAA surfaced publicly at a general meeting of the IAAA held in Dublin on 24 November. Sixteen delegates from eleven clubs attended, all but three of these from Dublin. The meeting was, however, dominated by two men not present at all — Croke and Cusack. The former, by persuading the GAA to drop its boycott rule, had put it up to the IAAA to follow suit. The latter in a public statement the day before the IAAA meeting, indicating that overtures would neither be made to nor received from that body, had effectively ruled out any possibility of a compromise between the two associations. What Croke thought of Cusack's statement one can surmise from events some months later.

Of eight speakers at the IAAA meeting, seven called for talks to be opened with the GAA on an amalgamation of the two bodies. All implicitly accepted that the GAA had come to stay, but (oddly) only one suggested lifting the IAAA ban. The remaining speaker, L. H. Christian, the assistant secretary of the IAAA, who had opposed the GAA from the start, was totally against a merger. Eventually, apparently influenced by Christian's prediction that overtures of the kind suggested by other speakers were certain to be rejected, a decision was taken that, instead of approaching Cusack, his co-secretary McKay should be asked if Cusack's uncompromising attitude had the backing of the GAA executive. The IAAA then adjourned to await clarification of the GAA's policy.

The GAA's answer was not long in coming. On 3 December, a week after the secretary of the IAAA, John Dunbar, had written to McKay to enquire if Cusack spoke for the GAA, McKay replied in terms even blunter than Cusack's. The GAA, he wrote, had never considered a merger; its policy was absorption, not amalgamation, concluding pointedly: '... it now remains for your association to say what it is prepared to do.' The IAAA's next move, decided at the adjourned general meeting on 8 December, showed how desperate its position had now become. After a humiliating withdrawal of the original 'quash' threat to the GAA, followed, however, by a lack of support for a call to end the IAAA's boycott rule, it was decided to appeal to a general delegate meeting of the GAA for a rejection of the unyielding lines of Cusack and McKay.

To this latest (and last) overture from the IAAA Cusack's reaction was predictable. It came in a nine-word letter on 11 December to Dunbar. 'I received your letter this morning and burned it.' Although the war lingered on for another couple of months, its conclusion was now inevitable. The adjourned first annual convention of the GAA at the end of February 1886 duly acceded to Croke's wishes and rescinded the boycott rule. As to amalgamation, the same meeting ended Dunbar's hopes, for a show of hands was enough to satisfy Davin that delegates were united in opposition to merging with the IAAA. In the end, the latter's almost unanimous lifting of its boycott rule a month later at its first annual meeting was almost a non-event. As will shortly appear, it had in fact been overshadowed by a new development inside the GAA.

The spring of 1886 should have been the climax of Cusack's career as an agent of reform in modern Irish sport. And so, indeed, it was in many respects. After a decade in the jungle of mid-Victorian Irish athletics, during which he had experienced ignorance, frustration, opposition, bigotry and hostility — even at times from men who admitted the soundness of some of his ideas on reform — the new association he had launched little more than a year earlier was now safely afloat.

The captain of this sturdy vessel was acclaimed by its crew at the first annual general meeting of the GAA when it re-assembled in late February 1886. Cusack's first annual report as the principal honorary secretary — effectively its chief officer — was unanimously accepted. Compared to the maximum of twenty-nine clubs of which the IAAA could boast at any time in its first year, the GAA had secured the affiliation of almost seventy clubs. When it is appreciated that many more clubs had simply not paid their fees before the meeting — a further fifteen did so shortly afterwards — it is safe to assume that the real total of clubs then actively involved in the GAA was in the region of a hundred, or between three and four times the strength on paper of the IAAA.

Largely through his skilful use of the columns of *United Ireland* and the *Freeman's Journal,* Cusack had defeated the concerted effort made by the IAAA in 1885 to wipe out the GAA. With the lifting in March 1886 of the IAAA's rule banning GAA athletes from its meetings, the odious exclusion system, originally introduced before 1884 by the AAA (of England), was ended. From now on, athletes from one body could take part in events controlled by the other, and given goodwill on both sides the politically-motivated divisive element in Irish sport, against which Cusack had for so long campaigned, would disappear.

All too soon, however, it became apparent that peaceful co-existence between the GAA and the IAAA could not so easily be achieved. The bitterness of the war of words waged during 1885 had left its mark on some of the principal antagonists, not least on Cusack himself. Obliged to face his opponents alone in Dublin because his executive was largely scattered throughout the provinces, he become more dictatorial in his style of management and resentful of criticism from any quarter. In particular, he could not tolerate what he felt was lack of support from his own colleagues, some of whom now began to question his capacity to pilot the GAA into calmer seas, or the wisdom of allowing him to do so.

Ominously, the first public indication that all was not well in the relations between Cusack and the other leaders of the GAA came from Cusack's old hate-figure, Edmund Dwyer Gray MP, the proprietor of the *Freeman's Journal*. Unfortunately for Cusack, Archbishop Croke, between whom and Gray a close friendship had developed in recent years, also became involved. Inside a few short months this formidable pair were between them to bring about the end of Cusack's regime as chief officer of the GAA.

Early in March 1886, in the Waterford town of Dungarvan, Croke replied, in emotional terms that must have delighted Cusack, to a welcome from the local GAA club. Bluntly expressing his opposition to any merger with the IAAA, this outspoken champion of the Home Rule movement warmly praised the nationalist bias of the GAA. Referring to its opponents, he concluded, 'We will beat them out of the field of manly exercise as we have beaten them out of the field of politics.'

A week after the Dungarvan function, a meeting in Nenagh of the North Tipperary branch of the GAA passed a resolution highly critical of the attidude of the *Freeman's Journal* towards the Association. In the same issue of that paper that carried a report of the Nenagh meeting, Gray, in a letter to his editor, denied all the charges made at Nenagh. He also hinted that Cusack was behind the Nenagh resolution, an allegation the accuracy of which Cusack was soon to admit.

The Nenagh resolution repeated and brought up-to-date Cusack's case against Gray. The *Freeman* had boycotted the GAA from the start; the *Freeman* had recently refused to publish a correction by McKay of a reported speech he had made; the *Freeman's* subsidiary, *Sport*, had refused to publish Croke's famous letter of December 1884. The *Freeman* (the Nenagh meeting alleged) had also falsely reported that Cusack had ignored the playing rules in a recent hurling match he had refereed, and finally it had both shortened and delayed publication of Croke's Dungarvan speech. Unfortunately for Cusack, the charge of delay was to prove incorrect and Croke himself was to confirm this publicly soon afterwards.

There was worse to follow; and again it came from Croke. After three days, with no retraction either from the North Tipperary board or Cusack, Croke published extracts from a letter he had received from Cusack. In language both defiant and offensive, Cusack repeated his allegation of Gray's hostility to the GAA and claimed that he could fully justify the charges in the Nenagh resolution. Then, in a reference to a recent confrontation between Croke and the Pope over the former's involvement in Irish politics, Cusack's letter continued bluntly, 'As you faced the Pope, so I will, with God's help, face you and Gray.'

Croke's reply to this challenge was immediate and two-fold. For the first time he explained in detail that he himself had been responsible for the delay in the *Freeman's* publication of his speech, having asked for an opportunity to read what he had said before it appeared in print. Accordingly, he pointed out, either Cusack was wrong or he (Croke) was a liar. Then, in what a century later sounds like a bullying tone, he went on to warn the GAA of his intention to discontinue his patronage if Cusack was to be 'allowed to play the dictator in its councils', to abuse all who disagreed with him and 'to keep the Irish athletic world in perpetual feud'.

In a cleverly argued article, clearly from its proprietor's pen, the *Freeman* in its editorial columns in the same issue put the case for Cusack's removal. A vicious personal attack on him claimed that his 'zeal was not tempered with discretion', that he had 'little control over ... an unruly temper', that he could not pick up his pen without abusing someone, and that he 'lacked the spirit of ... courtesy' necessary for the post. He was 'always treading on someone's toes, suggesting ignoble motives, and only happy when quarrelling'. If the GAA did not quickly find a new Secretary (the paper ended) Cusack would wreck it.

Reaction from different levels of the Association itself was quick and unanimous. Inside twenty-four hours, one of Cusack's co-secretaries (McKay) repudiated Cusack's letter to Croke. While insisting that it had not been authorised, he said he, too, had found the *Freeman* papers hostile to the GAA in its early days. But he agreed with Gray that Cusack should apologise. From Cork, Waterford and Dublin came letters or statements from clubs, either supporting Gray's article or demanding Cusack's retraction, or both.

The initial trickle of anti-Cusack letters or reports now swelled to a flood. From Cork, J. E. Kennedy, a vice-president, called on Davin to convene the executive to demand Cusack's resignation. From Sligo, P.A. McHugh, local Home Rule leader and secretary of that town's GAA branch, described Cusack's manner as aggressive, insolent, dictatorial and an obstacle to the spread of the Association. From Nenagh, one of the fourteen North Tipperary clubs repudiated Cusack's letter to Croke, but not the charges in the Nenagh resolution.

The *Freeman* for its part continued to pursue the matter in its editorial columns. On 25 March, a short article, which expressed satisfaction with the protests so far, added ominously that no further action was needed 'at least so far as the public is concerned'. The following day, commenting on a decision by Davin to call a meeting of the executive for April 6 'to consider the present position and future management', the editor hoped that the meeting could 'result in placing the GAA on a stronger, broader and firmer base than ever.' On 29 March, the formal notice of the meeting appeared, but under the names of Power and McKay only; Cusack still had not made a public statement on the crisis which his letter had provoked.

3

At first glance the meeting of GAA delegates in Thurles on 6 April, the first of three meetings in the next three months which together resulted in Cusack losing his post as secretary, seems to have been a success for him. According to T. F. O'Sullivan's account almost thirty years later, 'Mr. Cusack admitted that he had acted indiscreetly, and explained that he had not the remotest intention of being offensive to his Grace', whereupon 'the explanation was accepted by ... thirty-eight votes to thirteen.'

The *Freeman's* more detailed account gives a somewhat different picture, showing that O'Sullivan had unwittingly done Cusack (and several other speakers, too) less than justice. The meeting began with a report by McKay of a meeting which Davin, Bracken, O'Crowley, Power and he had had with Croke, who declined to comment on the disagreement with Cusack. Davin then invited Cusack to give his side of the story, whereupon Cusack gave an accurate account of what had happened, accepting responsibility for the Nenagh resolution.

Frankly admitting that the final sentence in his letter (that he would face Croke as the latter had faced the Pope) was indefensible on its own, he denied that the letter as a whole was offensive. Now, for the first time, he revealed that he had done his best to withdraw any insult offered by writing privately to Croke denying any such intention; by clear implication the latter had not replied. By way of mitigation of his blunder, Cusack also explained that he had not known that it was Croke who was responsible for the delay in publishing Croke's speech in the *Freeman*. Not only, Cusack concluded, had he never dreamt of insulting Croke; he had not, he argued, done so.

The reaction to Cusack's speech by the delegates representing sixty clubs was mixed. John Clancy of Dublin, recently appointed treasurer of the GAA and soon to fall out with Cusack, formally proposed that his explanation be accepted, with J.J. Kenny of the Metropolitans seconding. A Cork delegate moved a direct negative, calling for Cusack's resignation, with a Kildare delegate seconding. Another Dublin delegate urged that the whole matter be dropped if Cusack apologised. The resignation call was lost without a vote, whereupon a Cork delegate demanded a vote on the Clancy-Kenny motion, which was approved by thirty-eight votes to fourteen.

However, just before the meeting broke up, a curious proposal by O'Crowley of Cork (Cusack's critic of 1883) and Bracken (soon to reveal implacable hostility to Cusack) was approved, clearly without a vote and apparently without any overt opposition. This directed that all future communications made on behalf of the Association should carry the names of the president and of two of the three secretaries. It was Cusack's irrational response to this obvious attempt to silence him that was to cost him his post as secretary three months later.

Cusack's candid account of the April meeting to an American audience two years later is worth giving. 'In March 1886 I wrote a long and hurried letter to Dr. Croke ... complaining of the persistent hostility of ... Gray and of the *Freeman*. His Grace was offended, and he complained publicly of my too great readiness to fight everybody. An extraordinary general meeting was called to get me to apologise or resign. I would do neither, for I was not conscious of doing anything wrong, and notwithstanding ... the malignant attacks of my enemies, my expression of regret that a man whom I revered should have taken offence when none was intended, and my emphatic denial of having been guilty of any misconduct deserving of censure, won me 38 votes out of 52. But I was not to be let off so easily.'[5]

However, although Cusack's last sentence provides the key to much of what happened during his remaining three months as secretary of the GAA, his own impetuous temperament led him to walk into what may have been a deliberate trap set for him by his leading critics on the executive. For, instead of trying to carry on as chief officer or mending his ways, he chose to obey the letter rather than the spirit of the April meeting's final resolution. Far more obtaining (or even seeking) the necessary signatures to any letters, he simply wrote none at all. This naturally brought the whole administration of the GAA to a halt, and his own regime as secretary to an inevitable end.

By mid-June Cusack's conduct had so incensed his executive that Davin was persuaded to summon a special delegate meeting of the Association for Thurles on 4 July. Before that, however, a meeting of the executive (or of some members of it only, according to Cusack later) was held on 15 June in the Imperial Hotel in Dublin. Associated with this meeting, which set the scene for the proceedings in Thurles a fortnight later, were two prominent GAA figures who were to be vitally concerned in Cusack's dismissal.

L. C. Slevin was an Armagh man who had been closely involved with Cusack since the foundation of the Metropolitans. Recently appointed an assistant to Cusack to organise the Whit sports in Dublin, Slevin was to be an important participant at the Thurles meeting and a stern critic of Cusack's opponents. Also involved in the preparations for the Whit sports was John Clancy, a member of Dublin Corporation who was then assistant editor of the *Nation* and later a prominent Home Rule MP. Early in 1886, Clancy had been made treasurer of the GAA. Despite his support of Cusack at the April meeting, the two had become bitter enemies by July.

One cause (but not the only one) of the friction between Cusack and Clancy related to the financing of trophies for major sports. O'Crowley seems to have supported Clancy in his practice of purchasing trophies without prior approval from the executive. To

John McKay   *John Wyse Power*

make matters worse for Cusack, Wyse Power, between whom and Cusack friction has existed from the start, also supported Clancy. So serious had the breach between Cusack and the executive grown by 15 June that for the first and only time Cusack stayed away from an executive meeting.

When the meeting to consider Cusack's future as secretary began in Hayes's Hotel on 4 July, some sixty-five delegates representing almost forty clubs were present. Not surprisingly, twenty-four of the clubs and almost half of the delegates were from Tipperary. Representation was even more unbalanced, because while most clubs sent two delegates, ten had only one each. A request by Slevin for a formal roll-call (presumably to decide voting rights) was turned down.

From the executive itself there were three notable absentees — Davin, Clancy and Power. Davin's absence has never been satisfactorily explained, and the papers in his family's possession throw no light on it. Although it is easy to speculate that he was reluctant to preside over the expected dismissal of Cusack, the rest of Davin's presidency, in particular his two resignations from the post, suggests that he was not one to evade unpleasant decisions. As for Clancy and Power, while physically missing each had ensured that he was very much present in spirit at this vital meeting. According to a story published just over twenty-nine years later (at a time when he was still alive to challenge its accuracy) Power had come to Thurles to confront Cusack, but got cold feet and left before the meeting.[6]

After preliminary queries about the purpose of the meeting had been dealt with, McKay read two long letters from Power and Clancy setting out detailed allegations of incompetency against Cusack. He believed, Power's letter began, that the negligent manner in which the GAA's affairs were being conducted warranted immediate investigation. Although he had taken over control of the Association from the start, Cusack was now utterly neglecting its affairs. He was not (Power continued) dealing with correspondence, nor acknowledging affiliation fees received from clubs, nor issuing medals even for the previous season. As a result of Cusack's mismanagement the Association was suffering, especially because he (Power) and the other officers were having to spend much of their time apologising for Cusack's neglect of his duties as secretary.

Next McKay read from a similar letter by Clancy. He had, Clancy alleged, received no financial report from Cusack, nor replies to letters asking for it; only repeated insults. Although he made no reference to the disagreement with Cusack about trophies, he managed somehow to create the impression, without expressly so stating, that Cusack had pocketed some of the GAA's money. Although Cusack hotly denied this implication (which even his enemies in the IAAA had never made), it seems at least possible that it was a factor that influenced some delegates to vote against him.

Cusack's defence ran on predictable lines. Regarding the unanswered correspondence, he argued that he had a complete answer in the restrictions imposed on him by the April meeting. Then, going on the offensive, he explained the conflicting views of Clancy and himself on the purchase of trophies in such a way as to imply clearly that Clancy was guilty of improper behaviour. Finally, in a dramatic gesture of defiance, he answered the veiled accusations of embezzlement by producing a bundle of unanswered letters and uncashed cheques and throwing them all on the table in front of him.

For the executive, McKay and Bracken replied to Cusack's speech. Of the two, McKay was the more effective. He made a convincing case for the proposition that Cusack had all along been a dictator, never consulting either of his two co-secretaries, never answering McKay's letters and frequently being offensive to any officer who dared to disagree with him. Several minor speakers followed, among them Slevin and Molahan of the Dublin delegates, who defended Cusack.

The debate lasted for four hours, becoming disorderly at times and being also punctuated by at least two walk-outs by Cusack. In the end, the case against him for neglect of his duties was almost unanswerable, and on a proposal by William Fisher of Waterford, with John McGennis of the *Freeman's Journal* Athletic Club seconding, Cusack was (in the terms of the motion) 'asked to resign because he had not discharged his duties as secretary'. The voting was forty-seven to thirteen, with some three-quarters of the delegates against Cusack. The final indignity offered to him was a decision to ask *United Ireland* to end his weekly Gaelic column. 'Night had set in without moon or stars,' was Cusack's comment later.[7]

4

For the founder of the GAA this was an inglorious exit from a position of power in a body he had set up only twenty months before. Disowned, rejected, even (in Davin's case) shunned by those who had acclaimed his new sports association, Cusack remains over a century later the only leader of a national organisation in this country to be dismissed in modern times.

That his dismissal was fully justified is undeniable, for he had shown himself (especially since the April meeting) unfit to be secretary of the GAA. From the start he had been offensive, insulting and intemperate in language towards both opponents and colleagues. His colleagues in the GAA, who shared his ideals, he treated in much the same way as he had the officials (now all in the IAAA) who had opposed him before 1884. Moreover, it is safe to assume that in his personal contacts Cusack went even further than he did in print. In continuing to conduct controversies and to pursue vendettas beyond a stage when no useful purpose was served in doing so, he neglected what should have been his main concern in 1885 and 1886 — the spread of the GAA throughout the entire nationalist community.

Furthermore, the charge of incompetency made against Cusack in July 1886 by reputable figures in that body were not confined to the few months since the Dungarvan episode. According to McKay, the dozens of letters he had alleged had gone unanswered by Cusack referred to a period of six months before the Thurles meeting. Nor can the venom in McKay's speech there be satisfactorily explained by Cusack's conduct towards McKay over only a short period. The secretary portrayed in March 1886 by the reliable P. A. McHugh of Sligo as having 'hindered the spread of the Gaelic Athletic Association' because of an 'attitude uniformly aggressive ... insolent ... [and] dictatorial' was a Cusack McHugh had obviously experienced over a long period — probably since Sligo's affiliation in the autumn of 1885.

Even William O'Brien MP, the editor of *United Ireland,* who had encouraged Cusack to set up the Association then and given him the weekly column which became Cusack's most valuable propaganda vehicle, was obliged at least once to tone down Cusack's intemperate language, when Cusack's target was none other than Dywer Gray. One cannot avoid wondering, too, why on at least four occasions in March and April of 1886, and again only three weeks before the 4 July meeting, Cusack's article failed to appear. It may not have been a coincidence that the earlier of these two periods was also that of Cusack's confrontation with Croke, who counted O'Brien among his intimates as well as Gray.

Nothing, it is suggested, more clearly shows that the decision to dismiss Cusack was a correct one having regard to the interests of the GAA than the treatment accorded to the 4 July meeting by T. F. O'Sullivan. Writing at a time, only ten years after Cusack's death, when memories of the episode must still have been fresh in the minds of many in the GAA, he disposed of the proceedings in two short sentences. 'The meeting was specially summoned for the purpose of considering the manner in which Mr. Cusack had been performing his work as secretary. It was decided by 47 votes to 14 to dispense with Mr. Cusack's services on the grounds that he had not been discharging his duties satisfactorily.' The truth, but not the whole truth in any sense of that phrase, surely?

Yet, when the adequacy of the case against Michael Cusack is admitted, the manner of his dismissal still remains indefensible. It is not merely the absence of Davin, Power and Clancy that calls aloud for explanation. Davin's absence, after all, enabled Cusack's admirer Frank Maloney of Nenagh to chair the meeting, even though Cusack's own preference was Robert Frewen of Aherlow — a choice brusquely rejected by Bracken. As for Clancy and Power, the likelihood is that their presence might well have turned what was a fairly turbulent debate into a violent shambles. That this is what would have happened is suggested by the scene between Cusack and Bracken, when Cusack temporarily left the meeting on being called a liar by Bracken.

What strikes a reader of the various accounts of the Thurles meeting a century later as unsatisfactory, if not demonstrably unjust, about the manner of Cusack's dismissal is the one-sided aspect of the whole episode before and during the actual meeting. Two events, seemingly crucial to the decision taken at Thurles, were the 15 June meeting of the executive in the Imperial Hotel in Dublin, and the Whit sports, the first annual national sports of the GAA. Unfortunately, no full account of either has survived. Indeed, much of the scrappy information about both events is clearly partisan.

Since it was held the day after the Whit sports, one would expect the Imperial Hotel meeting to have discussed that event. Yet Slevin, who had recently been appointed an assistant secretary specially to organise the sports, was refused admission to the hotel according to Cusack, whose assertion that others of the executive besides himself did not attend either was never denied. As a result, one is left with the suspicion that the sole purpose of the Imperial Hotel meeting, convened perhaps hurriedly before the executive dispersed after the previous's day's sports, was to finalise plans for the Thurles meeting two weeks later, at which Cusack was to be removed from his post as Secretary.[8]

A similar cloud of secrecy hangs over the Whit sports. Although subsequently publicised as a major success for the GAA, not only Cusack but several delegates at Thurles and sections of the sporting press were critical of some of the arrangements. According to Slevin, so seriously did Clancy take these criticisms that he offered his own resignation after the sports — and, after all, he gave up his post before the end of the year in any event, on his election as an MP for North Dublin. What seems certain is that Clancy's inexplicably sudden hostility towards Cusack dates from the Whit week-end — whether as a result of the sports, a public disagreement between the pair in a Dublin club on the Friday evening, or the clash with Cusack over the trophies, is not clear.

As for the Thurles meeting itself, the press accounts when taken together read more like a public trial of Cusack rather than an impartial investigation of his regime as secretary. At an early stage a suggestion by Bracken to limit speakers to five minutes each was accepted, despite a protest by Cusack that he could not present his case in such a short period. Although it seems clear that Cusack got plenty of time to answer the case made against him, the debate also appears to have been dominated, if not monopolised, by delegates hostile to him. Some of these, according to Slevin, continuously interrupted Cusack — to such an extent as to suggest to Slevin a pre-arranged plan to do so. However, Cusack himself also managed several timely interruptions of his opponents' speeches.

Several speeches, nearly all from the vocal delegates representing six Dublin clubs, tried to put forward compromise solutions aimed at averting or postponing a decision on Cusack's future that day. A couple of speakers argued against a decision on the grounds that the purpose of the meeting had not been notified to delegates beforehand. One delegate advised that, even if Cusack was guilty of negligence, it would be impolitic to dismiss him just then. Two Tipperary delegates suggested that in future Cusack (who by implication should be allowed to stay on as secretary) should be required to reply to every communication to him inside three days.

However, the feeling of the majority was manifestly against Cusack, even though he drew occasional applause. W. G. Fisher of Waterford defended the absent Clancy, and matters apparently reached a climax when Cusack walked out in protest against the chair allowing Bracken to call him a liar. Discussion on Cusack's conduct as secretary continued in his absence, but he apparently returned in time for the vote, in which he presumably participated, since only twelve delegates were listed as having supported him. Of these, two each were from the Davitts, Faughs and Metropolitan clubs of Dublin, two each from the Moycarkey and Aherlow clubs of Tipperary, and one each from the Drapers Assistants Club (Dublin) and the Nenagh Club (Tipperary). However, the Tipperary support for Cusack was counter-balanced by the unorthodox behaviour of Maloney in vacating the chair to vote against Cusack — a gesture that led to a lifelong feud between the two.

By far the most extraordinary aspect of the accounts of the Thurles meeting, however, is the absence of any reference to a new breach that had recently developed between the executive of the GAA and its secretary, and which was totally unrelated to his conduct as secretary. Since March, Cusack, alone of the GAA leaders, had refused to agree to a new policy of co-operation with the IAAA, apparently decided on as a direct consequence of the lifting by that body of its ban on participation at its meetings of GAA athletes.

One is struck, for example, by the fact that although the meeting lasted four hours, even the longest published report of it would hardly account for one hour. One is forced to wonder if the three papers concerned (the *Freeman, Sport* and *United Ireland*) suppressed the portion of the proceedings relating to this fundamental change of policy by the GAA. That relations with the IAAA were not discussed at all is inconceivable; on the contrary, an otherwise inexplicable accusation by Slevin about the inadequacy of the press reports may be interpreted as implying that this vital topic, so clearly tied in with Cusack's duties as secretary, was in fact discussed.

It was, after all, hardly a coincidence that these three papers were controlled by either Gray or O'Brien, of whom one was hostile to Cusack and the other had had difficulty passing Cusack's weekly contributions for publication. It goes without saying that none of the leading Home Rule personalities indirectly affected by Cusack's removal — Gray, O'Brien, Croke — publicly shed any tears over his dismissal.

What lay behind this change of policy by the GAA, which its secretary was not prepared to go along with, can now only be guessed at in the absence of minutes of the executive, which have survived only from 1898. Until early in 1886 the Association had, after all, rejected suggestions from the IAAA that the two bodies should co-operate on the management of Irish athletes. As recently as its adjourned annual convention in February 1886, the GAA, led by Davin, had, without even the formality of a vote, turned down a merger. Moreover, Croke himself had also come out forcefully against such a union; and Cusack had always been against it.

Yet the evidence for such a change of attitude towards its rival body is clear, if not abundant. It emerges first from several statements by Cusack. As late as the day before his dismissal he warned his readers in *United Ireland* that he was not prepared 'to hand over the Gaelic Athletic Association to the enemies of Irish sport'. Also, that some form of co-operation between the GAA and the IAAA had actually commenced is evident from the holding, in the early weeks of the 1886 season, of meetings jointly sponsored by both bodies or (where cycling events were included) between the GAA and the ICA. The *Freeman's Journal* A.C. annual sports in late May was held under the joint auspices of the GAA and the ICA, and the Drogheda FC sports around the same time under the joint auspices of the GAA and the IAAA.

Moreover, the existence of some support for this policy of co-operation between the GAA and its rival would go some length to explain both the hostility between Cusack and Power, and the return to GAA involvement of the latter. From the start there had been friction between these two. Cusack later alleged that Power had wanted to pull out of the GAA at an early stage. When he was in the witness box in mid-1885, Cusack had made a barbed reference to Power's inactivity as an officer of the Association. At Thurles on 4 July 1886, it became clear that Power had not in fact been involved in GAA activities until the previous spring. It may be recalled, too, that it was Power who, as far back as the GAA convention of October 1885, had put forward a suggestion for some form of agreement between the GAA and the IAAA. Finally, it ought perhaps not be overlooked that from early 1885 or so Power had moved from Naas to join the staff of the *Freeman* in Dublin.

To Cusack, of course, such a fundamental reversal of his policy on the management of Irish athletics was unthinkable. He referred to it as effectively co-operating with those whom he had opposed for a decade. It would mean allowing into the GAA the very people, to exclude whom from any influential voice in Irish athletics he had founded the Association. Little wonder that he complained bitterly at Thurles that he had found his fellow-members on the executive refusing to work with him in recent months.

In these circumstances, it is easy to see why Cusack had to go. He had now become the only obstacle to the GAA executive's implementing its new policy of co-operation with the IAAA. Whether the other GAA leaders would have tolerated Cusack's irresponsible behaviour for much longer is irrelevant. What is relevant, and what they must have found so convenient for their purpose, was that this same behaviour provided them with a ready-made pretext for prising him out of his post as secretary. Little wonder that his most loyal supporter, Slevin, one of those who had begun the second hurling revival in 1883, was not allowed to join the caucus in the Imperial Hotel — at which, one suspects, the formalities for the Thurles meeting were finalised.

There remains, finally, one major unanswered question about the Thurles meeting: Why did Davin stay away? Unlike Power and Clancy, he could plead neither business nor distance. He, after all, could easily have left his farm in the capable hands of his brothers for one day to travel the thirty odd miles to Thurles. There is one clue. Alone of the executive, Davin is not on record as having supported closer relations with the IAAA. On the contrary, at the convention in February 1886 he had not even put the idea of a merger to a vote. It is possible that he was unhappy about the new policy — and unhappier still about taking part in the removal of Cusack over it?

Footnotes
1. See *FJ*, 29.10.1887.
2. *The GAA in Louth* (Rev. J. Mulligan, 1984), p. 4; *Rathkenny GAA History* (Mongey, Mongey & McBride, 1985), p. 11.
3. *CT*, 25.6.1887.
4. *Irish Athletic & Cycling News*, 1885-86.
5. *Chicago Citizen*, 22.9.1888.
6. *Gaelic Athlete*, 10.7.1915.
7. See n. 5.
8. *CT*, 17.12.1887.

Principal Sources
Freeman's Journal, 1885 and 1886
Irish Athletic & Cycling News, 1885 and 1886
Irish Sportsman, 1886 and 1886
O'Sullivan, T.F.; *Story of the GAA* (Dublin, 1916)
Sport, 1885 and 1886

CHAPTER EIGHT

THE CITIZEN IN DECLINE

1886–1906

Although he was to live for over twenty years after his dismissal as secretary of the GAA, Michael Cusack was never again a major figure in the Association. He did, however, retain an active interest to the end in Irish games and athletics, and in the body he had founded to promote them. But, as from the end of the proceedings in Hayes's Hotel in Thurles on the afternoon of 4 July 1886, he ceased to be a force to reckon with in Irish sport. Having been deprived of his power base in the GAA because of dissatisfaction with his performance as secretary since November 1884, Cusack became almost overnight a person whose views on hurling, football and athletics no longer counted with those controlling those pastimes.

Furthermore, it at once became clear that his former colleagues in the GAA not only intended to disregard Cusack but also proposed actively to ensure that his views on the Association would, if they could help it, no longer be publicly aired. As for Cusack himself, the realisation that he was no longer in a position to influence the GAA took a long time — perhaps some ten to twelve years — to accept. Indeed, for at least eighteen months after his rejection by the GAA he tried, first by private overtures and then through a costly public medium, to regain his influence over GAA policy.

Nevertheless, astonishing though it may at first appear considering the manner of his dismissal, Cusack and the GAA never parted company. For the rest of his life (or at least whenever he surfaced from relative obscurity) he remained immersed in its activities. Mostly he turned up either as a sideline spectator (and often a noisy one too) and usually at club level, now and again as a club delegate for one of several Dublin clubs at county board meetings, and frequently either as a delegate or an honoured observer at the annual congress, but rarely getting as far as the executive or central council. Always, too, he would argue (or at least clearly imply), as he had done all through the 1886 crisis in the

GAA, that in everything he did or said or wrote in relation to Gaelic games and athletics, his sole concern was the welfare of the body he had set up in 1884. And, in his own eccentric way, he was usually telling the truth, if not always the whole truth.

On reflection, of course, Cusack's continued participation in, and loyalty to, the association, from the chief post in which he had been so brusquely displaced, was neither illogical nor surprising. After all, ever since his arrival in Dublin in 1874 he had worked towards the establishment of a body such as the GAA. For him to have abandoned, much less opposed, the GAA, in spite of what he clearly regarded as its many and serious shortcomings in the period of twelve years or so after his dismissal, would have been totally out of character.

Indeed, in these circumstances it would have been more surprising were Cusack to alter or moderate the strength of his criticism or the power of his invective, even when directed against recent colleagues and associates on the executive. On the contrary, in the years just after July 1886 his pen seemed at times to release a new venom not evident when he held the post of secretary of the GAA. It was as if, now that he was free from previous restraints, whether imposed by loyalty to the Association or dictated by O'Brien's watchful editorial eye in *United Ireland,* Cusack felt free to heap on those guiding the GAA's policy much the same kind of abuse he had hitherto reserved for his enemies in the IAAA and the *Irish Sportsman.*

Not only in the years after 1886, but also well into the 1890s, Cusack was only occasionally in tune with many major aspects of GAA policy. Indeed, to those trying to formulate and administer that policy the criticism continually being directed at them by their founder must have seemed often negative, and at times largely destructive. Furthermore, Cusack's views must also have seemed frequently more hurtful because the actions of some of his former fellow-members on the executive of the GAA — the resignations of Davin, the changes of sides by Bracken and Wyse Power, the departure of McKay, to mention only a few — somehow suggested that some of his criticisms may have contained some validity.

In addition, what from time to time gave some of Cusack's less eccentric or less bitter views an air of authority was the fact that he never seemed to lack some minimal degree of support inside the GAA. There seemed always to be some club in Dublin anxious for him to represent it on the county board; often, too, that county was willing for him to represent it at congress. In addition, he continued to take a sincere, if at times a misguided or distorted, interest in the GAA, participating in its outdoor activities, particularly handicapping and refereeing.

Gradually, as he approached middle age, Cusack mellowed in some important respects, and even for a while seemed to drop out of, or to lose interest in, GAA affairs. In time he became reconciled to, and later supportive of, the role the Association was beginning to play in the new nationalist movement from 1900 onwards. Correspondingly, a younger generation taking over in the GAA — many of them prominent in a re-activated IRB, whose members had been among Cusack's most bitter opponents in the late 1880s — came to look on him as a kind of father figure. 'I am luxuriating in the manful enjoyment of those who have taken my place,' he explained towards the end of the 1890s to the founder of Sinn Féin, Arthur Griffith.

This visible, indeed easily detectable, change in the relations between Cusack and the GAA — from a position of often bitter and illogical hostility in the late 1880s and early 1890s to one of almost patronising, or at least benevolent, support in the closing years of the century — coincided with a gradual decline in his own personal fortunes. Family bereavements, a scarcity of teaching opportunities, and a loss of journalistic income all had an effect on Cusack the private individual, and were also accompanied by poor health. Although outwardly he seemed to make little of this decline, he became even more eccentric in his habits, becoming an obvious target for caricature-portraits by James Joyce and Oliver St John Gogarty, neither of whom knew the Cusack of twenty years earlier. From the late 1880s onwards, Cusack became one of the 'characters' of Dublin city, the burly maverick figure who, from his own habit of addressing his friends as 'Citizen', became himself widely known as the Citizen Cusack.[1]

For almost the whole of the second half of 1886 there is no record whatever of Cusack, until shortly before Christmas. For the first time in many years the Dublin newspapers are without any reference to him — no letters from him, no participation by him in athletics or Irish language activities, none of his usual advertisements announcing the successes of students of his Academy. Indeed, so far as reports of GAA events, both indoor and out of doors, for this period are concerned, he might as well have ceased to exist overnight.

All this is, of course, no more and no less than one might expect in the circumstances. Ironically, although Cusack's opponents in the athletics movement had failed for ten years to silence him, his own former colleagues in the nationalist athletic body he had set up only twenty months earlier now succeeded in doing so in days. Denied any further space in *United Ireland* by O'Brien at the behest of the GAA executive, just as surely barred by Gray from the *Freeman* and its subsidiary *Sport,* and (one may safely assume) by James O'Connor from Pigott's *Irishman* and by John Clancy from the Sullivan's *Nation,* Cusack now had no outlet for his views on Irish sport, or on anything else for that matter.

Predictably, yet surely to his credit, Cusack resisted the temptation to seek space in some of the other sporting organs, in particular the *Irish Sportsman,* which at the end of 1886 complimented the GAA on its staying-power during the previous two years. So what Cusack's reaction was to McKay's resignation as secretary in August or O'Crowley's as handicapper in October is not known. As to the sudden appearance of Gaelic games columns in *Sport,* the *Irish Sportsman* and the IAAA organ *Irish Athletic and Cycling News,* between the autumn of 1887 and January 1888, one may only surmise that these developments caused Cusack a mixture of pleasure and cynical disbelief.

But, if the absence of anything by Cusack in any nationalist (or other) newspaper from July to December 1886 suggests that he was idle, there is evidence that he was not. First, there is that all too often overlooked and curious sentence in his last published letter (in *United Ireland* of 10 July 1886), less than a week after his dismissal. This indicated his intention not to give up, but rather to make arrangements for another general meeting, at which (he hoped) the GAA would be forced 'to declare for or against national pastimes'.

Admittedly, no such meeting took place, presumably because the executive simply would not hear of it. But almost thirty years later came the revelation, by one who was close to the Sinn Féin element then dominant in the GAA and a friend of the surviving founders, that twice towards the end of 1886 Cusack had offered to act as adviser or guide to the Association, only to find his overtures understandably rejected. Thirdly, there is the account from the same source (Séamus Upton, editor of *Gaelic Weekly*), hard to accept had it not been for supporting evidence from Cusack himself, of a meeting between Cusack and P. N. Fitzgerald in, of all places, the *Freeman* office in December 1886. Wyse Power, an unwilling spectator but also a loyal employee of Gray, had Cusack ejected, not for the first time, from the premises.[2]

So what had begun as his most successful year ended with the apparently complete eclipse of Cusack as an influential figure in Irish sport. Yet outward appearances can be deceptive, and it seems likely that both the GAA and the IAAA knew before Christmas of 1886 that the founder and ousted secretary of the GAA was about to put his own distinctive imprint (in the literal sense, too) on Irish sporting journalism — perhaps spurred on by news Cusack may have picked up about moves by some of the GAA executive to start a weekly organ of the Association.

2

On 1 January 1887, the first issue of a new Irish weekly sporting newspaper appeared.[3] Although the masthead of the *Celtic Times* stated that its editors were Michael Cusack and A. Morrison Millar, even a cursory glance at the contents of almost any surviving issue shows that Cusack was effectively the sole editor. Upton, who had reliable sources of information on the period, describes him as editor-in-chief. Destined to last for only fifty-four issues, the *Celtic Times,* not a single issue of which had been seen by the public for at least the fifty years from 1934 to 1984, deserves its own special place in Irish sporting history.

This long lost (and still generally unavailable) paper was the first of many periodicals which have been devoted to Gaelic games in the past hundred years or so. Since he had played no editorial role in the *Gaelic Journal,* the *Celtic Times* was the only paper of which Michael Cusack was in sole control. Moreover, even allowing for some input by Morrison Millar, the paper reveals a new side of Cusack for long unknown, or at least only vaguely suspected from his other writings. This hidden Cusack was a man not only with a broad liberal approach to the economic and cultural development of his country, but also with a lively interest in social and labour problems both at home and abroad.

To students of the formative period of the GAA, Cusack's *Celtic Times* is, of course, of particular value for several reasons. It enables one to give a portrait of the founder of the GAA largely unseen before, not available elsewhere, and not at all as unbalanced as one might have expected in the circumstances giving rise to the

·Let· ·Native· ·Industries· ·Literature· ·Arts· & ·Pastimes· ·Flourish·

The Celtic Times

VOL. 1.—No. 44.   DUBLIN, SATURDAY, OCTOBER 29, 1887   Registered for Transmission Abroad.   PRICE 1

Industrics.

HELPS AND HINDRANCES.

The fact that industries have only a limited life strongly impresses itself on thinking men. Almost every change in the social condition of a people either kills or creates an industry, and not unfrequently a change is calculated by the generality in whose midst it occurs. The introduction of gunpowder did away with the manufacture of bows and chain armour, and quite accurately, though more indirectly, terminated the feudal tenure of land. Who could have foretold such wide and deep changes from the mixing of sulphur, charcoal, and nitre? Help to the advance of peaceful industries not seldom comes from unexpected quarters; but no matter where the aid comes from, the Captains of Industry should be prepared to utilize it. The Rev. Patrick Bell was a divinity student when in 1827 he invented the reaping machine, and it was only ten years before this when John Loudon Macadam published his "Practical Essay on the Repair and Preservation of Public Roads," one of the most practically useful works ever issued, and when three years later he macadamised the Bristol road he performed a work second only to that which Appius Claudius did for Rome in 188.

The disgraceful condition of the roads and streets of the countries and cities of Christian Europe, which necessitated the use of pack horses, were in striking contrast to the paved streets of Cordova, and the well-laid roadways of the Western Caliphate under Abdurrhama the II. in 850, whose care for the bodily welfare of his great Commonwealth reached to a pitch of excellence that as yet we are struggling to attain. At first these changes were unnoticed. Bell's machine lay unregarded until the first great exhibition in London, and some Americans saw the potentiality for good of the machine, and the making of agricultural machines occupies to-day thousands of skilled workers. There is no more doubt but that circumstances certainly produce a man capable of dealing with difficulties than there is that circumstances mould animal form; for the existing circumstances mal-adamizing was as certainly produced by circumstances as any event in history. Its essential purport was the facilitating of intercourse by making it more safe and rapid, and the necessity for regular, safe, and rapid communication between Ireland and England during the period of the Commonwealth caused Cromwell to re-establish packet boats to ply weekly between Waterford and Milford and Chester, and by his ordinance of 2nd September, 1654, appointing John Manley postmaster, he established virtually our present postal system. The advantages were unrecognised during the licentious period of the Re-storation, and the House of Hanover was too wrapped up in the welfare of Germany to give a thought to the peoples of these islands, and not until

Title page of Cusack's newspaper, the Celtic Times

launching of the paper. It provides a new account of what was the most eventful year in the history of the GAA, from the pen of probably the most articulate and most observant side-line spectator. Finally, but by no means of least interest, it shows the Association's dismissed chief officer fighting back — making what was to prove his last bid to regain power in the body he himself had set up.

The influence on the *Celtic Times* of Morrison Millar, a prominent Scots businessman in Dublin and founder of the Caledonian Society in the city, is evident in several important respects. However, most of these were of a technical rather than an editorial nature, although for that reason they must have helped to make the paper the commercial success it appears to have been for much of 1887. Which of the two editors was responsible for the tabloid size of the eight-page weekly cannot now be stated, and one can also only guess to whom to give the credit for the attractive green four-page cover which usually contained the bulk of the more substantial (and presumably the more expensive) advertisements.

The most surprising feature of the advertising material is its range and variety, considering that the *Celtic Times* was a publication concentrating mostly on sports supported almost exclusively by the nationalist community. In many issues there were large display advertisements from reputable foreign concerns, among these (predictably) Scottish insurance companies. In the case of the mostly smaller, but even more frequent, advertisements by Irish firms, these came almost entirely from advertisers of whom it is safe to say that they were not likely to be supporters of Gaelic games.

Every issue of the *Celtic Times* contained an offer, to readers filling in a simple form, of a free insurance policy from a Scottish company. Among advertisers still (or until recently) flourishing in the Dublin area were Thomas Henshaw the ironmongers, Dollards the printers, Kean & Co the accountants, the General Accident Assurance Corporation, and Sibthorpe the sculptors. Some prominent Irish hotels regularly took notices in the paper, as did several leading veterinary surgeons and other periodical publications. Another frequent advertiser was the famous Dublin bookseller, Michael Hickie, known to his customers as 'Tricky Mickey Hickie'.

If Morrison Millar's contribution to the *Celtic Times* was confined to the technical aspects of the paper, then Cusack is revealed as having a whole range of interests extending far outside the purely cultural sphere. Almost weekly he argued the case for Irish industry in terms anticipating by over a decade the views of Arthur Griffith, the founder of Sinn Féin. Ways in which hitherto neglected native resources could be developed were explained; new industries were encouraged and public support for them pleaded for; the suppression of once thriving Irish industries by British misgovernment was recalled, with the obvious implied moral that it was now time to revive them since (as was widely believed in 1887) Home Rule was a distinct possibility in the near future. Since Cusack and Griffith became close friends on the latter's return from Africa in 1899, it may well have been from Cusack that Griffith got his policy on protectionism, only abandoned in the 1970s by Seán Lemass.

A long article entitled 'Encouragement of Native Industries' in the *Celtic Times* for 26 February was followed by several articles on cottage industries on 12 March, 19 March, 2 April and 16 April; there had also been one on 1 January, a missing issue. On 16 August a long well-argued editorial made the case for the revival and development of Irish fisheries, a source (Cusack claimed) of great potential wealth that had never recovered from the Famine decimation of the population along the western coast. Financial aid, he insisted, would be required to improve harbours and to provide rail outlets instead of existing costly freight services. Government intervention was urgently needed — from London, until an Irish Government took over on the winning of Home Rule.

On 20 August an editorial headed 'Support Home Industries' made a convincing case for a 'Buy Irish' campaign of the kind still considered necessary a century later. Not only (Cusack insisted) should his readers support small Irish industries, but they should also use only Irish goods in their daily lives. They should wear only Irish clothes, wash them with Irish starch, and start their fires with Irish matches only. No clearer evidence of the importance he attached to this topic can be adduced than his publication, free with the issue of 13 August, of a special four-page supplement, containing a talk on the Irish flax industry given to the Irish Industrial League and the United Trades Council in Dublin by Professor C. H. Oldham of Trinity College, the secretary of the Irish Protestant Home Rule Association.

Nor was Cusack content to preach in general terms the merits of Irish industry, without giving some examples from new or existing industries to prove his point. Almost every second issue of his paper contained an account of a particular industry or trade that, in his view, deserved public support. Some of these accounts are so detailed that they required considerable research, mostly in Dublin but also elsewhere, and they reveal his skill as an investigative reporter. Among the industries he dealt with were flour milling, iron galvanising, brush making, paper manufacture, poplin weaving, tobacco growing, antique jewellery, printing and photographic processes, bottle and glass making, shipbuilding and cork cutting.

In addition, almost every issue of the *Celtic Times* shows that Cusack was keenly aware of the need for good labour relations. He was a staunch champion of bodies of employees such as trade unions and trade associations, and a forthright supporter of the individual rights of employees, whether organised or not. As a corollary of these advanced views for his time, Cusack gave prominence in his paper to the activities of trade councils and also to the rise of international bodies representing organised labour. He appears to have been present at the first meeting in Dublin in March 1887 of a new body called the National Industrial League that had international links.

Yet his sympathy with what a later age would call the proletariat did not prevent Cusack from singing the praises of big business, especially where it conferred benefits on the Irish economy. In March, for example, he paid a visit to Belfast — his first time in Ulster for thirteen years — and he returned impressed by the impact on that city of the industrial revolution. He did not hesitate to disagree publicly with the Dublin Protestant Home Rule MP, Charles Dawson, on industrial policy. Dawson believed that little could be done to promote Irish industry until self-government was achieved. Cusack took the opposite line, and was gratified to observe that his view was shared by the new Archbishop of Dublin, Dr William Walsh, a committed nationalist.

That Cusack should take an interest in the ideas of an American economist may at first seem surprising. But Henry George of Philadelphia, who twice ran for the mayoralty of New York, was no ordinary economist. 'Single Tax George' had become world-famous for his theory of a tax on land values in substitution for all other taxes, put forward in 1879 in his best-seller, *Progress and Poverty*. Two years later he published a book on the Irish land problem and visited Ireland for Patrick Ford's influential paper, *Irish World*.

On this side of the Atlantic Henry George's views were taken up by Michael Davitt. To him the core of the American's theory — the confiscation of rent by including it in a land tax to be used for the benefit of all — naturally appealed as a solution to the agrarian problem here, although it seems that Davitt under-estimated the difficulty in applying George's idea to Ireland. Davitt and he became firm friends, and George became a useful champion of the Irish agrarian cause abroad.[4] Doubtless the fact that George's wife, Annie Fox, an Australian, was of Clare and Limerick extraction did not escape Cusack's notice.

Cusack's treatment of Henry George showed editorial shrewdness. He first mentioned George in the context of the 1886 New York mayoral election, which George lost to the corrupt Tammany Hall machine, but in which he ended well ahead of the future president, Theodore Roosevelt. Then, in an age when nationalisation was a dangerous topic, he linked his support for the American economist with the views of the liberal American Cardinal, James Gibbons of Baltimore. Gibbons, the son of a Mayo man, helped to ensure tacit Vatican approval of the American labour movement and was also influential in preventing the American bishops from condemning George's reforms.[5]

As might have been expected from one coming from humble origins and who had supported the cause of the under-dog in Irish athletics for some twelve years, Cusack's writings on industrial topics show a strong bias in favour of the employee. The tenth issue of the *Celtic Times* carried a long article entitled 'The Future of the Workingman', with a pro-trade unionist flavour throughout, and welcomed the recent setting up in Dublin of a Central Executive Trades Council. Two weeks later, in an article headed 'The Workingman and his Friends', Cusack returned to this theme, again coming out strongly in favour of trade unionism. Nine months later an editorial, clearly from his pen, dealt with the topic 'Only a Working Man'.

Cusack's paper regularly carried reports of the activities of trade union bodies, at a time when such proceedings received scant publicity in Irish newspapers. Among the organisations the *Celtic Times* covered were the Dublin Trades Council, the Dublin United Trades Council, the Irish Industrial League, the National Labour League, the Operative Bookbinders Society and the Dublin Workingman's Industrial Co-Operative Societies. In addition, Cusack published American Labour Notes and gave prominence to a sophisticated argument by a Scottish contributor to what a later age would describe as a form of Christian Socialism.

Education and literature were not neglected by Cusack. In an early editorial he put forward a scheme for parish libraries, to be controlled by local committees representing priests and teachers. He also wrote on the need for greater recognition in the Irish educational system of the role of physical education. Literature appeared in several forms. Although a column he began for Irish poetry was not a success, he persisted with it and also published Irish translations (sent in by readers) of well-known Irish ballads.

The *Celtic Times* also made sporadic efforts to provide its readers with some of the fringe features then common in newspapers. Although music and cookery received scant treatment, notes on chess, veterinary matters and agriculture lasted for several months, and he even secured a serial story. Outdoor sports (other than those of Celtic origin) were not touched on, American football receiving similar treatment from Cusack to that given to the first films of Australian Rules in Irish newspapers a century later. Shinty (the Scots version of hurling) and bowls (then not, as now, confined to Cork) got more favourable coverage. Cusack offered a challenge trophy for a game between hurlers and shinty players that was not to materialise in the brief lifetime of his paper.[6]

As was to be expected, the principal topic dealt with in every issue of Cusack's paper was Gaelic games and the body that promoted them. The GAA and its policy and future were, after all, the *raison d'etre* of the *Celtic Times*. But for his dismissal and his inability to find an outlet for his views on Irish sport after that, his paper would never have appeared in Dublin newsagents' shops on New Year's Day of 1887. Whether its appearance did the Association any good is, it will be suggested, doubtful; and the paper was to prove a personal disaster for Cusack himself. Nevertheless, one must be grateful for the fact that the issues that have survived for over a hundred years enable one to give a more detailed portrait of Cusack than has hitherto been possible.

For fifty-four consecutive weeks Cusack filled the greater part of his paper with news and views of the GAA. Yet it is unlikely that his decision to launch the *Celtic Times* was prompted by rumours that must have reached him in the autumn of 1886 of a proposal to start an organ of the Association. Almost certainly his plans had passed the point of no return by the time of the turbulent encounter in the *Freeman* office towards the end of 1886, when P. N. Fitzgerald rejected Cusack's latest overture.

When it came to reporting GAA events and meetings Cusack was, of course, seriously handicapped because he could only publish accounts of events he had witnessed himself or reports sent in by readers or supporters. Since all his rival publications were hostile to him, Cusack could not follow the then customary practice of 'lifting' their material or even re-writing it. But on many occasions his resourceful pen found ways of getting factual information into his commentaries on the affairs of the GAA in 1887.

It was probably because of his need to obtain up-to-date information, and also to muster support for his paper, that Cusack made several trips into the provinces during 1887. In addition to the Belfast visit already mentioned, he twice visited Meath (where he found the GAA machine hostile to him) and also Tipperary town once. His report on that town threw some light on the dual allegiance to Gaelic and rugby so skilfully skirted round by T.F. O'Sullivan thirty years later. There was also a prolonged visit to Clare with his wife, which seems to have produced little worthwhile for his paper.

An equally serious handicap from which Cusack suffered for most of the life of the *Celtic Times* was his inability to publish detailed (often, indeed, any) reports of the proceedings of the GAA executive. Yet, so wide-ranging were the editorial comments and other notes on events in the Association during 1887 that the loss to the reader (who would in any event have read accounts elsewhere, too) is more apparent than real. Moreover, as matters moved to their climax in the GAA in the autumn of 1887, Cusack clearly decided that he had to take risks and borrow material from his rivals. As for the historic convention in Thurles in November, the *Celtic Times* account is as full as any appearing elsewhere, despite the fact that its editor had, in effect, fled the town the night before the meeting in unusual circumstances soon to be described.

Given these different restrictions implicit in running a weekly paper single-handed and against hostility from his rivals both on the GAA executive and within the *Freeman* group, Cusack managed surprisingly well to give his readers a picture of the state of the Association during 1887. He not only made skilful use of material supplied by supporters, but when recalling his own regime as secretary managed to make obvious comparisons with 1887. He showed his continuing concern for hurling by offering a cup for competition to be confined to clubs west of the Shannon. At least a year before the GAA executive seriously adopted the idea, he initiated the debate on a project to send a team of hurlers and athletes to the United States. The first article on this topic, an anonymous one by Cusack entitled 'An Invasion of America', appeared on 21 May and drew support from Davin's brother, Pat, and from Dan Fraher of Dungarvan, a prominent figure in the early GAA.

Predictably, Cusack also used the *Celtic Times* to renew hostilities with the *Freeman*. At least three times he told of how *Sport* in 1883 excluded reports of his hurling games every Saturday in the Phoenix Park. He also told of his ejection from the *Freeman* premises early in 1884 on the orders of the editor. Finally, in the issue of 13 August, he accused the *Freeman* management of trying in the spring of 1884 to get him to change his allegiance from *United Ireland* to *Freeman* publications, and repeated his old allegation that soon after the foundation of the GAA all the *Freeman* publications had boycotted the Association on the instructions of its editor, Gray.

It was, of course, with the broad general policy of the GAA in 1887 that Cusack was mainly concerned in his new weekly paper. It was, after all, according to himself, mainly because he disagreed on a fundamental point of policy that he had been dismissed in 1886. It was inevitable therefore that he would use the editorial columns of the *Celtic Times* to try to influence GAA policy. Whether, and to what extent, he succeeded in this aim — whether, in short, his paper had any effect on the course of events in the Association's council chambers in 1887 — remains to be seen.

The sequence of events on the GAA executive in the second half of 1886 has been adequately traced twice recently, both in broad outline and in some detail, and can also be followed from the selective pen of T. F. O'Sullivan. After the ousting of Cusack the Fenian element on the executive strengthened its grip on the GAA, meeting little opposition from Davin, whose sympathies were with the Home Rule camp. Yet signs of friction between Davin and his IRB colleagues on the executive had begun to appear even before the end of 1886, and by the start of 1887 control had passed to the Fenians. Pat Hoctor had become vice-president; John B. O'Reilly had succeeded Cusack as secretary, and the recently returned Fenian leader, John O'Leary, had been added as a fourth patron.

All this meant that by the time Cusack launched his paper the situation confronting him was quite different from that which had existed at the time of his dismissal six months earlier.

Although IRB members such as Bracken and Wyse Power had been among his severest critics, it was against what he felt was the Irish Party intrusion led by John Clancy that Cusack had made his stand in the months before his dismissal.[7] With Bracken and Power, after all, opposition to him was largely based on personal grounds. With those for whom Cusack believed Clancy to speak he joined issue on a vital policy matter — whether or not to co-operate with, perhaps even to accept into the GAA, some of those non- or anti-nationalist athletics officials he had been at loggerheads with for ten years or so.

By early 1887, however, the Irish Party dominance of the executive, which Cusack had probably correctly judged was responsible for his dismissal, was gone. Instead, the GAA was now effectively being run by an IRB triumvirate — Hoctor, O'Reilly and the Corkman P. N. Fitzgerald. In these circumstances it would now be logical for the new paper to support the new executive. This was, in fact, the line Cusack took (if in a largely negative way) and adhered to in the *Celtic Times* well into the autumn of 1887.

For a person with such an independent mind as Cusack, it was, of course, only to be expected that events and personalities would occasionally stretch his support for the new executive beyond breaking point. His instinctive dislike of O'Reilly, whom he regarded as quite incompetent, increased month by month. The new secretary became a regular object of anonymous jibes in Cusack's weekly column 'Harmonic Rays', where he concentrated his strongest criticism of what he felt was the disastrous way GAA affairs were being run since his dismissal. However, the vicious personal tone of the *United Ireland* of 1886 was largely missing from the *Celtic Times* of 1887. Instead, he was usually content to ridicule O'Reilly, who was thinly disguised in Cusack's paper as 'Baffetty', a reference to O'Reilly's humble position in Clery's drapery store, baffety being a type of coarse cheap cloth than widely used for men's clothes.

From the early summer of 1887 Cusack switched his attack to Hoctor, who, from the appearance in April of the unauthorised organ of the executive, *The Gael*, was, as its editor, Cusack's competitor. Since only one complete issue of this paper has survived, all one can say about its treatment of Cusack is that it seems that Hoctor, an impulsive and often unscrupulous figure, at least gave as much as he got from Cusack in the latter's paper. Yet as late as 2 November Cusack was protesting that until a few weeks earlier he had stood by the executive, and the surviving issues of his paper justify this claim.

As the spring of 1887 gave way to the summer, the actions and policies of the executive caused growing concern to Cusack. By November he was openly expressing disagreement with the election of John O'Leary as patron a year before, pointedly observing that previous patrons had been invited to act, rather than being elected by the executive. At his meeting in December 1886 with P. N. Fitzgerald, Cusack had divided the GAA into two parties which had developed since his dismissal, 'an ... unscrupulous party' acting in concert with the *Freeman* and 'an honest but incapable party' playing into the hands of their rivals. This shrewd summary was to be proved all too accurate before the end of 1887.

Yet, astonishingly, there was not a line of criticism from Cusack of the extraordinary decisions taken by the executive of its 24 February meeting. In flagrant breach of the constitution (as Davin later pointed out), it altered the rules so as to give more power to the newly formed county committees, and through them to the executive itself, whose nominees could now dominate any (or every) county committee. Cusack's tacit acceptance of this fundamental change in the GAA's administrative structure is all the more surprising since he himself was opposed to county committees, a view he adhered to for many years despite Davin's conversion later in 1887 to the merits of decentralisation and local control.

At the next meeting of the executive (on 21 April) it became clear that the decisions of the 27 February meeting were not acceptable to Davin. Oddly, however, not even after reports of the April meeting appeared did Cusack take up his pen to protest, much less to support Davin in his stand against the rest of the executive, with whom he was now at loggerheads over the vital issue of the management of the GAA. Yet as far back as November 1884 Cusack was aware of the danger of the Association coming under the control of one section of the nationalist movement. In an article in his paper on 19 March he explained that at the foundation of the GAA the patronage of Parnell had been sought in order to remove 'the danger of the GAA being antagonistic to the National League'.

Just how out of touch with events on the executive Cusack had become is shown by a short commentary of his in the *Celtic Times* for 30 April. After expressing dismay at the lack of any response by Davin to the executive's policy of decentralisation, Cusack went on to criticise Davin for his continued silence. Yet, although he only made the news public six months alter, Davin had in fact resigned the presidency a week after the 11 April meeting. He had, he explained in November, concluded that in the interests of unity this course was preferable to the alternative one of calling a special delegate meeting to discuss (and hopefully to reverse) the executive's changes to the rules at its February meeting.

It was not in fact until mid-May that Cusack realised that Davin had resigned almost a month earlier. From then on he took up enthusiastically the cause of the Association's first president, to whom of course he was deeply indebted since the summer of 1884 for his prestigious support in founding the GAA. Now at last the *Celtic Times* had a major and clearcut editorial issue on which to differ from its rival, *The Gael*. For the next six months Cusack persistently called for the return of Davin; this he regarded as essential, if the body they had jointly founded was to survive and the national pastimes it had begun to preserve were to prosper.

On 21 May, the first issue after his discovery of Davin's resignation, Cusack published a well-reasoned article 'Maurice Davin's Resignation', signed by himself. Recalling the course of events that had led to the resignation, Cusack expressed the fear that it would 'render the Association into fragments'. In sober language he wound up by suggesting that a general meeting of clubs be called to consider the matter. This course Davin later confessed he had rejected because of its likely divisive impact.

As if hoping for some reaction, Cusack now allowed two months to pass without any further direct reference to Davin. All the evidence suggests that there was no contact between the two. In the meantime, on 18 and 25 June he published in full the rules of the GAA, so that any observant reader could readily see the extent to which the executive had departed from the position obtaining before Davin's resignation. Then on 9 July, in his 'Harmonic Rays' column, he at last took an openly anti-executive line when he came out against the identification of the GAA 'with the party of extreme violence'.

Almost every week from then on Cusack left his readers in no doubt about his support for Davin. On 23 July, in one of his frankest comments so far, he alleged that Davin had resigned because of O'Reilly and Hoctor. On 3 September, he gave prominence to a letter from Archbishop Croke regarding a current dispute between an influential Dublin club and the executive, in which Croke smartly rapped the executive on its knuckles. The next week Cusack himself was critical of Frank Dineen, a future secretary and president now coming into prominence, who because of his IRB membership was a supporter of the executive.

On 24 September a signed editorial by Cusack entitled 'Storm Signals' forecast serious trouble ahead for the GAA at the convention due in November. A week later, in the 1 October issue, in another article signed by Cusack, he named Gray, Hoctor, O'Reilly, J. E. Kennedy of Cork and Bracken as those sailing the Association into troubled waters. On 8 October, in another signed article headed 'The Morning of Battle', Cusack directed most of his fire at O'Reilly, and the following week's signed article, 'Breakers Ahead', aptly summarised the warnings he had been giving for the benefit of delegates to the convention.

With, as was then assumed, only two weeks to go before the convention, the *Celtic Times* on 22 October launched a two-pronged attack on the executive, now well advanced in its plans for an IRB take-over of all the key posts, in which Davin would be replaced by Fitzgerald. An editorial headed 'The Good Ship Gaelic' praised Davin as 'a grand old sailor, whose courage and devotion to his gallant charge preserved her from mishap', but who 'was soon thrown overboard by the treachery of the recruits whom he had invited to join him'. Then, in a piece of invective reminiscent of some of his more vitriolic comments in *United Ireland* in 1885, Cusack lashed out at the executive and at its organ — 'the organ of incompetent dictators ... of spiteful hypocrisy ... of foulness, meanness and absurdity ... of idiocy and illiteracy ... of spurious patriotism, and ... of all that is mean and contemptible.'

After this outburst the last two issues of the *Celtic Times* before the convention returned to more sober language and wiser tactics. On 29 October an unsigned editorial, clearly from Cusack's pen and headed 'Mr. Maurice Davin', calmly repeated the case for the president's return, a letter from whom also appeared in the same issue. On 5 November Cusack lifted from the *Freeman* two long letters of his own which that paper had recently published, and a full report of a long interview which the *Freeman* had had with Davin, who gave his version of the events of the previous six months. In an editorial Cusack analysed this interview, in a last attempt to persuade uncommitted delegates to the convention of the soundness of Davin's case.

Since the proceedings of the famous convention in Thurles courthouse on 9 November 1887 have been adequately dealt with elsewhere, no detailed account is called for here. Suffice it to summarise events by stating that, led by P. N. Fitzgerald, the Fenians so dominated the meeting that a sizeable rump of delegates walked out and held a rival meeting outside Hayes's Hotel. The majority elected their own nominee, Edward M. Bennett of Clare, to the presidency and then filled all the executive posts with their own supporters. Yet, complete though it seemed to be, the Fenian take-over was to be of short duration, at least in the short term.

Because he was not present, we have no account of the convention from Cusack. Travelling down from Dublin the previous night to cover the meeting for his paper, and as a Dublin delegate, he found his presence unwelcome to the executive. When he tried to insist on his right as a journalist to attend, he was accosted and physically threatened by Hoctor and O'Reilly. In Hayes's Hotel a pistol shot was fired at Cusack — whether by Hoctor or someone else is not clear — as a warning to leave the town. Realising the futility of remaining on, and fearful for his own safety, Cusack took an evening train back to Dublin — where presumably he felt he could more usefully serve Davin's cause by preparing the next issue of his paper.

The following month's issues of the *Celtic Times* showed that Cusack had not given up the fight for Davin. On 12 November, three days after the GAA had (by a vote of doubtful validity) displaced its first president by a delegate largely unknown outside of Clare, the paper devoted most of its issue to a verbatim report of the convention. The following week Cusack published in full Davin's plan to reconstruct the GAA; it was by then clear that a wave of support for him was sweeping through the Association at club level. In a short, anonymous and moderately worded article Cusack contented himself with a call for Davin's return.

In his next two numbers Cusack continued to campaign for Davin, whose ideas for reform of the GAA were by now widely supported. The column 'Harmonic Rays' for 26 November was headed 'The Thurles Packers', a reference to the sizeable proportion of spurious delegates at the convention. In an anonymous editorial came the revelation by Cusack that the anti-Fenian Fr Scanlan was of Clare Fenian stock, his father having been in the abortive Fenian Rising of 1867, one brother of the priest having had to flee to the United States and another having been imprisoned for similar activities that same year.

It soon became clear that, while working independently of Davin,

Croke (who had withdrawn his patronage after the convention) had also taken the initiative to heal the split in the GAA. By early December, Davin had joined representatives of both sides at the archbishop's residence in Thurles; the new executive was now resigned to the return of Davin. Against this background Cusack, by now again fully in touch with events, permitted himself on 3 December the luxury of an article headed 'Gone to Canossa', while also reproducing in full an important letter from Croke to the *Freeman*. For once Gray and Cusack had identical interests.

By 10 December, when (under an agreement reached between the new executive and Davin's supporters) arrangements were in train for county conventions to elect delegates to a general meeting (the 'reconstruction convention') to be held after Christmas, Cusack's tone had become positively triumphant. 'Once more the grand old ship has got her captain, and the captain his loyal lieutenants'. The following week he published Croke's explanation of the reconstruction proposals, while on an opposite page (in a final and anonymous contribution) Cusack recalled the decline of the GAA during the preceding eighteen months. Abandoning all pretence at moderation or objectivity, he claimed that 'the seeds of the disease' were sown in Dublin on 14 June 1886 (the date of the Imperial Hotel meeting which he had declined to attend), and that what he called 'the rash' had broken out in earnest on 4 July 1886, the day the general meeting in Thurles had removed him fom his post as Secretary.

In his mood of elation over the impending restoration of Davin at the reconstruction convention (due on 4 January 1888) Cusack now claimed that he and his paper had played a major role in the overthrow of the Bennett executive only two months after its election. One's initial impulse is to marvel at Cusack's audacity; after all, he had taken no part in the talks so skilfully supervised by Croke. It is, indeed, an indication of how permanent and total Cusack's rejection eighteen months before had been that all three parties involved in these talks — Croke, the IRB and the Davin party, including Davin himself — had their own good reasons for excluding the founder of the GAA from their discussions.

Yet Cusack's claim to the contribution the *Celtic Times* made to Davin's reinstatement cannot be summarily dismissed. Not only the many letters his paper received in its early months, but also favourable comments expressed on his paper at some county conventions before the Thurles convention, suggest that Cusack was still not without some degree of grass-roots support during 1887. Moreover, the persistent and moderately-worded campaign which the *Celtic Times* had mounted to bring Davin back certainly did the first president's cause no harm — even if Davin never publicly admitted as much. On the other hand, once Croke came on the scene after the Fenian take-over, with the clear intention of reversing the convention's capture of the executive posts, Davin needed no support from Cusack.

Finally, it remains only to explain the apparently sudden demise in mid-January 1888 of the *Celtic Times,* and at the same time to challenge the hitherto accepted explanation of this event. Because *The Gael* and Cusack's paper ceased publication at more or less the same time, and because this occurred soon after the January 1888 convention, it has been assumed for a century that the two events were connected. As far as *The Gael* was concerned there can be little doubt that its disappearance was a direct consequence of the overthrow of the Bennett executive. Davin, after all, like Cusack, always challenged the right of *The Gael* to call itself the GAA's official organ, so it can be safely presumed that he would not have countenanced its continued publication.

No such consideration, of course, applied to the *Celtic Times,* which was a private venture launched by Cusack and Morrison Millar. One needs little imagination to guess what Cusack's reaction would have been had Croke or Davin suggested that, now that the GAA was again united, Cusack should cease publication. It would, after all, have been in character for Cusack to continue; one would have expected him to have gone on for many months of 1888, alternatively gloating over the defeat of the Bennett executive (and doubtless boasting of his role in that triumph) and welcoming the return of Davin to the presidency. Instead, however, only two weeks after Davin's re-election Cusack's paper suddenly ceased to appear.

What had happened was simply that Cusack's paper had failed to pay its way. On his own admission, its circulation had fallen from 20,000 a week in May to 10,000 in December. Around Christmas a last-minute attempt to rescue it was mounted, in the shape of an invitation to supporters to take up a share-issue of 2,000 £1 shares, so as to convert the venture into a limited company. When this appeal met with no response, the number due for publication on 21 January 1888 was abandoned — in all probability because the printers refused to carry on until earlier bills were paid. A story, told a quarter of a century later, of a final dramatic gesture by

Cusack, who is said to have pawned his watch to raise funds, suggests that the *Celtic Times* had only barely struggled on to see the end of the GAA split and Davin's return.

3

Whatever doubt there may have been as to Michael Cusack's impact on the GAA while his *Celtic Times* lasted, there can be none at all about his status *vis-a-vis* the Association once his paper collapsed. As from mid-January 1888, despite occasional attempts by him to give a different impression, Cusack became a minor figure in the GAA; and a minor figure he remained to his death almost nineteen years later. In that sense, the end of the *Celtic Times* was also the end of the story of Cusack and the GAA.

That he quickly got back into the Association, that he continued to work for (and usually inside) the GAA for the rest of his life, and that he retained a genuine interest in its success and in the spread of the pastimes it promoted — all this can be conceded without qualification. But so fundamental were the differences on major GAA policy between Cusack and the ruling body of the Association after 1887 that he never again succeeded in holding any office of importance in it. Nor is there any evidence that at any time after 1887 those in charge of the GAA took any serious notice of the Association's founder.

It is true that twice (in 1883 and 1901) Cusack seemed to be close to making a come-back in the GAA. It is true, too, that by the time of his second attempt he appeared to be at last more or less in tune with the role which the central council (as the executive had now come to be called) was then playing in nationalist affairs. But on both occasions Cusack failed to obtain or retain an important post in the Association. Moreover, if (as will shortly be suggested) his near-success in 1901 was more apparent than real, Cusack found himself in his last years in the position of a symbolic father-figure, to whom little more than formal respect was accorded. It is in this light, it is suggested, that an event like his visit to Belfast in 1904 to help re-establish the GAA in Antrim should be viewed, and it is surely significant that the trip seems to have been no more successful than a similar one he had made ten years earlier.[8]

Mainly as a result of the bitterness of the Parnell split of the previous few years, which had undermined the whole nationalist movement, the fortunes of the GAA in Dublin were probably never at a lower ebb than in 1893. Yet even then a handful of prominent members, determined to keep the ailing Association alive, were working, often feebly but always doggedly, towards a revival of what had by 1890 became one of the most active county boards of the GAA. The last thing such men — prominent among them Frank Dineen, P. P. Sutton and the GAA secretary until 1892, Pat Tobin — wanted just then was a split in the Dublin county board.

Yet that is precisely what happened suddenly in 1893; and all the evidence now available points to the conclusion that the person wholly to blame was Michael Cusack. At the annual Dublin convention in March he headed the poll in the election for secretary, getting sixteen votes to thirteen and three for two other candidates. His rivals, while maintaining that he could not take office because he had not obtained a majority of the votes cast, were unable to agree among themselves on how to proceed. When Cusack's supporters naturally insisted that his election was valid, the convention broke up in disorder, apparently when one faction refused to consider advice offered by Tobin, who was present. The obvious device of eliminating the third candidate and holding a second ballot between Cusack and his nearest rival could not, it seems, be countenanced by Cusack's opponents, since it was (to them) reasonable to assume that in the likely event of a tie the chairman, J. J. Kenny, one of Cusack's oldest friends from the 1883 revival, would give his casting vote for him.

What happened after the convention broke up suggests that suspicions of Kenny's impartiality were well founded. For Cusack, continuing to assert that he had got a majority decision in his favour, simply took over as secretary with the apparent connivance of Kenny. For at least six months he proceeded to run the affairs of the GAA in Dublin in much the same dictatorial style as he had run the entire Association before his dismissal in 1884. By the autumn of 1893, however, reaction to his take-over had been so decisive that the GAA in Dublin had practically ceased to exist — just what his opponents in 1886 had predicted would have happened to the GAA as a whole had they not then removed him from office.

However, in the divided state of the GAA in 1893 the central council failed to act as decisively as had its predecessor in 1886. Yet it had plenty of evidence that support for firm action would be forthcoming if this were done, for by the summer of 1893 some two-thirds of the thirty-four or so Dublin clubs had withdrawn their affiliations from the Dublin board and had made it clear that they would not return so long as Cusack remained as secretary. In July, the anti-Cusack clubs sent a deputation to the central council, protesting against the illegal regime and calling for action. Cusack insisted on getting a hearing, too, from the council, which then ruled that his election had been invalid and directed the board to hold fresh elections inside a month.

Cusack's response was predictable, if drastic. He simply disaffiliated the Dublin board from the council, which thus found itself unable to enforce its July decisions. But (not for the first time) Cusack had gone too far; his support now began to fall off, presumably as the prospect grew of Dublin's exclusion from inter-county competitions in 1894. One suspects, too, that Tobin did some discreet lobbying for the council. It was hardly a coincidence that, just before the date in October fixed for a special meeting of Dublin clubs, a majority affirmed their loyalty to the central council.

There was still some fight left in Cusack. Although the October meeting set up a provisional board of fifteen to function until the next convention in November, the latter had to be postponed twice to February 1894, so that by then almost a whole year had elapsed since Cusack's take-over. Even then, it seems, a complete purge of Cusack nominees was not carried out, for at the next Dublin convention in November 1894, in a move probably planned by the central council, Tobin took over as chairman from Kenny — to whose club (Erin's Hope) Cusack had recently transferred for obvious reasons.[9]

Cusack comes badly out of this whole affair, which halted for two years the recovery of the GAA in the city and surrounding area.[10] Even his friends at the time thought so. The then Parnellite organ, the *Irish Daily Independent* alleged (on 21 October 1893) that Cusack, a fanatical supporter of the dead "Chief", was motivated by party considerations — in other words, that he could not countenance the departure by the Dublin board from the strong Parnellite stance it had maintained since 1890. One suspects, however, that P. P. Sutton, a former colleague of Cusack in the Metropolitans in 1883 and now in charge of the Gaelic column in *Sport*, was nearer to the truth. He said that it was simply personal ambition that had motivated Cusack — presumably his way of saying that Cusack had hoped to use the Dublin board to regain power in the GAA.

Even more revealing is the treatment of this year-long Dublin GAA split by T. F. O'Sullivan, a lifelong admirer of Cusack, when twenty-two years later he came to write the first history of the Association. In a blatantly partisan account, he incorrectly stated that the episode had ended in October 1893, omitting any reference to Cusack's blocking of the convention fixed for that month. O'Sullivan then went on to report two Dublin conventions for 1894, disguising the fact that the earlier one was the real end of Cusack's revolt, and not the first of two Dublin conventions for 1894.

T. F. O'Sullivan's distorted record of the 1893 episode is of interest for another reason. When, eight years later at the historic GAA congress of 1901, Cusack made what from contemporary reports looks like another attempt at a come-back in the Association, the principal actor in the curious drama (apart from Cusack himself) was the then youthful secretary of the Kerry board, T. F. O'Sullivan. Again an attempt was made to falsify the record. This time the culprit was Frank Dineen, the former secretary and president of the GAA, who overlooked the possibility that the minutes of the congress would be available to contradict his account.

When on 22 September 1901 over forty delegates and officers of the GAA assembled in Hayes's Hotel for the annual convention, the Association was fighting for its very survival. For the third successive year a convention of the GAA had been postponed for the same reason; no financial statement was ready to go before the delegates. For reasons not material here, the GAA had failed to exploit the upsurge in nationalist sentiment that had followed the countryside celebrations, three years before, of the 1798 rising. The number of home counties represented at the 1901 congress (eight) was the same as in the previous two years, compared to thirteen in both 1897 and 1898, when the GAA was regarded as being on the road to recovery after the Parnell split.

This time, however, the prospects for the GAA's future were brighter. A small group of mostly younger men (all of whom would soon be identifiable as adherents of the new Sinn Féin movement) had for over a year been quietly working to build a new Association. One of their ideas — the decentralisation of GAA administration through provincial councils that would raise extra income — had been accepted by the 1900 congress. For a year or so now, the new Leinster Council, chaired by Kilkenny's Jim Nowlan, had been reviving disorganised or moribund county boards in its area.

Apparently frustrated by the lack of co-operation from older men like Dineen, the reformers now decided that the two big posts of president and secretary had to be captured if their plans were to make further headway. Since the president, Michael Deering of Cork, had died six months earlier, they knew that the chair at the forthcoming congress would be occupied by one of the leading reformers, Nowlan. Long before the meeting began he had been privately selected to contest the presidency, with another prominent reformer, Luke O'Toole of Wicklow and Dublin, being chosen to challenge Dineen for the secretary's post.

The election of Nowlan as president was unanimous. The election of O'Toole as secretary did not go so smoothly, however. First Dick Blake of Navan, a controversial secretary from the mid-1890s, was proposed. Before a seconder came forward Nowlan asked for a show of hands, as Blake had not participated in GAA affairs since his dismissal in 1898; Blake was rejected. Then, with T. F. O'Sullivan proposing and a London delegate seconding, Cusack's name was put forward. On a ballot, O'Toole, who had been sponsored by two other Dublin delegates, beat his fellow Dublin delegate, Cusack, but only by two votes — nineteen to seventeen.

Given the careful preparations that had preceded the vital capture of the two posts by the reformers, Cusack's high poll nearly deprived them of their double coup. Yet the temptation to regard this as a near come-back by him only four years before his death should be resisted. Granted that the search for the truth is hampered by skimpy central council minutes and inaccurate press reporting, other explanations of Cusack's apparently good performance deserve consideration — and are, it is suggested, to be preferred to the come-back theory.

First, while O'Sullivan's motive for putting up Cusack can now only be guessed at, not too much importance should be attached to the London delegate's support. For a start, the O'Sullivan remembered by journalistic colleagues in Dublin as recently as the 1950s had a most persuasive manner. In any event, the seconder, Tom Semple of Thurles, whose reputation rests deservedly on his captaincy of the famous Thurles Blues when they won two All Ireland hurling titles in the following nine years, was in 1901 still a quite obscure figure in the GAA. Indeed, when he and O'Sullivan attended the 1901 congress they were aged only nineteen and twenty-one.

It is true that Cusack had given his support to the plans (starting with the new provincial councils) to rebuild the GAA, and it is understandable that the group planning the 1901 coup would have welcomed the support of the GAA's founder. But there is no evidence that the reformers had taken Cusack into their confidence, and his inherently unpredictable personality, as well as his image in contemporary Dublin (even if grossly exaggerated by Joyce and Gogarty) would have deterred them from doing so. How then did Cusack come within two votes of preventing O'Toole's election as chief officer of the new GAA?

One possible explanation of O'Sullivan's sponsorship of Cusack is simply that O'Sullivan was opposed to O'Toole. He may, for example, have felt that the election of O'Toole and Nowlan would give disproportionate representation to Leinster in a body hitherto dominated by Munster. Although the reformers included prominent Munster men like Dooley (Cork), Cummins (Tipperary) and Moynihan (Kerry), it is clear that most of the impetus for reform had come from Nowlan, O'Toole, Watt Hanrahan and Nicholas Cosgrave, the last two from Wexford.[11]

Often, of course, in otherwise inexplicable cases of this kind there is an even simpler explanation. One recalls, for example, the persistent oral tradition in Thurles as to how the RIC officer McCarthy came to be present at the foundation meeting of the GAA in 1884. He had known both Davin and Cusack from athletics; he just happened to be in Thurles on 1 November; he met one of them in the street or in the hotel and was invited into the historic meeting. Similarly, in 1901 Cusack (perhaps not knowing of the plan to put up O'Toole) may have asked O'Sullivan to propose him, whereupon the latter may have found himself unable to refuse. This theory at least has the merit of explaining Dineen's curious treatment of the meeting in *Sport*.

Even if one discounts the caricature of him by Joyce in *Ulysses*, the most favourable picture of Michael Cusack around 1900 suggests that his election as secretary of the GAA in 1901 would have been a disaster for an association then struggling to stay alive. With no permanent home and no steady income, widowed for many years, his family apparently scattered between relatives and institutions, he frankly admitted in January 1900 that he was no longer a prominent member of the GAA — surely the first prerequisite for a serious candidate for the post of Secretary?[12]

Moreover, it is extremely doubtful if Cusack's failing health would have permitted him to perform properly as secretary of the GAA just then. Only nine months after the 1901 congress his closest associates in the GAA in Dublin gave his physical condition as a reason why, now that he was 'far advanced into the evening of his life', he should be helped to retire to his native Clare.[13] What appears to have been the last photograph of Cusack (published three years after his death) clearly shows that he had prematurely aged, at least in appearance. The long white beard and snow-white head suggest a man well into his 70s, rather than one still in his early 50s.[14]

The Cusack of this photograph is surely the Cusack remembered by James Joyce when he left Ireland for good in 1904. When early in 1907 he read in far-off Trieste of Cusack's death, Joyce asked in a letter home to his brother Stanislaus if he had seen where 'old Cusack' had died.[15] Nor is it a coincidence that this was how Cusack was remembered by a Wexford delegate to a GAA meeting in Hayes's Hotel in 1902. At this — whether in the course of a fracas or as the result of horse-play is not clear — Cusack suffered a fall from a chair. Many years later the Wexford man, when describing the incident to his son, referred to 'the old man' falling to the floor.[16]

Moreover, in assessing the genuineness of the apparently impressive ballot for Cusack in 1901, one cannot ignore the fact that to many in the GAA (in particular to members more senior than O'Sullivan) he remained a controversial, not to say, a divisive figure. Less than a year after this congress, friends of Cusack in the Dublin GAA organised a testimonial to collect funds to enable him to spend his last years in Clare. However, this touching gesture was not adopted officially by the central council; it got no support from any unit of the GAA; and an exhaustive search of both Clare and Dublin newspapers suggests that it was a failure.[17] In addition, when at the 1905 congress O'Toole sought approval for a £50 grant for Cusack, the idea produced both a proposer and seconder for a motion to refuse such a grant, and on a vote five delegates went so far as to dissent openly from O'Toole's proposal.

That such a man was seriously considered as a candidate for secretary of the GAA in 1901 must, it is urged, be doubted. For some reason or reasons that can only be guessed at almost ninety years later, neither the press reports nor the minutes told the whole story of the 1901 congress. In addition, had Cusack been a serious contender in the contest with O'Toole, O'Sullivan would never have disposed of the incident as briefly as he did fourteen years later in his history of the GAA. He would at least (as the format of his book shows) have included it in his summary at the start of his chapter on 1901.

Similarly, Dineen in *Sport* was anxious to play down Cusack's apparently unexpected bid for power. A week later, in the Gaelic column of that paper (of which he was now in charge since the death earlier in 1901 of P. P. Sutton), he concealed the truth by stating that in the Cusack-O'Toole ballot 'many delegates did not vote'. Fortunately for Dineen, it was not then the custom to publish either the names of the numbers of delegates from each county. Otherwise readers who did their sums would have at once caught him out — as does O'Toole's record in the minutes of the congress.

Examination of the minutes produces the following results. County delegates totalled thirty-four, *ex officio* central council members present eight, with three others (J. Burke, W. Hanrahan and F. Dineen) belonging to neither cateogory. Of this maximum of forty-five, thirty-six voted for Cusack or O'Toole. However, the nine unaccounted for presumably included Nowlan (who as chairman would have only voted on a tie), and certainly included Bourke of Tipperary, who is listed twice — in the *ex officio* group and among the three 'others'. Accordingly, despite Dineen's assertion in *Sport,* a maximum of only seven abstained. Furthermore, if the seven included Cusack, O'Toole and Blake, and if Nowlan and Bourke are excluded from the forty-five, then only four may have abstained out of a maximum of forty-three — hardly justifying Dineen's 'many delegates' in *Sport.*

4

The collapse of the *Celtic Times* was not only the end of any hope Cusack had of regaining a position of influence in the GAA. It also marked the beginning of a decline in his personal position, such as to suggest that he had committed himself financially to the commercial success of the weekly paper, and had perhaps even taken undue risks in relation to the venture. In any event, with its failure things now began to go generally wrong for him. 'Misfortune dogged his steps through the later years of his life,' was Arthur Griffith's later comment.[18]

The first casualty of the collapse of the *Celtic Times* was Cusack's Academy. It cannot be a coincidence that from December 1887, the month his paper got into serious financial trouble, all trace of the Civil Service Academy vanishes. Considering the demands which editing a weekly paper must have made on his time, the wonder is that he was able to keep his Academy going during 1887.

Yet the regular advertisements he inserted in the *Celtic Times* prove that it was not only still flourishing almost to the end of 1887, but also that Cusack's pupils were still taking top places in various public examinations.

However, by early 1887 — perhaps even before that — Cusack was no longer residing or teaching in Gardiner's Place. From the spring of 1887, if not earlier, he had moved to North Great George's Street, only a hundred yards or so away. This transfer to a house nearby, but much less spacious than his Gardiner Place premises, suggests that, probably to launch the *Celtic Times*, he had by the autumn of 1886 effected certain economies which necessitated the move. It was, indeed, to prove only the first of up to half-a-dozen addresses Cusack was to be found at in the next sixteen years, and it is clear that those he occupied from 1890 or so onwards were lodgings rather than a home in the normal sense.

By September 1890 the Cusacks had moved again, for when in that month Cusack's wife, then aged only thirty-five, died, the family were residing at Goldsmith Street. A month later, his eight-year-old daughter also died, leaving him, now a widower almost in his mid-40s, with six children ranging in ages from thirteen to seventeen years. The two surviving girls appear to have gone to live (probably with relatives) in England, the four boys ultimately being placed in orphanages in Dublin.

With his Academy permanently closed, it seems that Cusack thenceforth had to rely on journalism for an income. Effectively his main earnings derived from his weekly educational column in the *Shamrock*, which lasted into the early 1900s. When shortly after the turn of the century this regular source of income dried up, Cusack apparently had no other income. According to a few of his intimates on the Dublin county board, by 1902 he was enduring privation, and when he died in 1906 he was almost penniless.[19]

Considering the way William O'Brien had cut off the Gaelic games column in 1886 on Cusack's dismissal as secretary of the GAA, Cusack must be considered fortunate not to have lost his *Shamrock* column too, since this was also controlled by O'Brien. However, in his weekly feature Cusack was careful not to stray outside the strict confines of educational advice. Indeed, comments of a political, or even of a patriotic, nature are few and far between in Cusack's *Shamrock* column from 1886 onwards.

Considering the drastic change in his private life which occurred in the years just after his paper colapsed, it is perhaps surprising that Cusack continued to interest himself at all in national pastimes. On the other hand, with his Academy no longer flourishing and with his children no longer residing with him, Cusack probably now found himself with time on his hands, especially after 1890. Not only did he keep up his interest in Gaelic games and athletics, but he also began once more to take part in the language revival movement, particularly in the years just after the foundation of the Gaelic League in 1893.

So far as the GAA was concerned, he concentrated principally on the affairs of the Dublin county board, where (as the 1893 episode showed) he came gradually to acquire his own following. Yet even here it is evident that his views, or more likely the abrasive way he expressed them, produced disharmony. This is surely the only conclusion one can draw from the number of Dublin clubs Cusack seems to have moved into and out of again from the early 1890s onwards — the Rapparees, the Erin's Hopes, the Hibernians, the Michael O'Dwyers, to name only a few at random. Equally significant is that the fact that, having resigned (for what reason is not clear) from the original Metropolitans in 1887, he did not re-join the club when it was revived in 1889.

With no outlet for his views after the demise of the *Celtic Times,* and no longer holding any post either on the GAA executive or (except in 1893, as already explained) on the Dublin board, there remained only the annual convention (or congress) for Cusack to use to make an impact on Association policy. Then, as today, congress was the great annual parliament of the GAA, at which major decisions were handed down to the central council and its officers to implement. However, it hardly needs to be pointed out that, if or when Cusack was at odds with the Dublin board, he was unlikely to be elected as a delegate to congress. On at least one occasion — in 1905, by which time he had become more or less acceptable to most of the central council — opponents were quick to exploit a technicality to prevent Cusack from representing a county (this time Wicklow) willing for him to represent it.

Of the sixteen annual conventions or congresses held between January 1888 and Cusack's death sixteen years later, he attended seven. Of these, five were congresses of the new GAA of the twentieth century, counting the 1904 congress (from which he was excluded) as one he attended. The other four were those for 1901, 1902, 1903 and 1905. At the 1902 congress (also attended by John McKay, home after many years in London) Cusack does not seem to have spoken at either session. With his son John he was again a Dublin delegate in 1903, the sessions being on 8 November and 13 December. Here he supported a motion by T. F. O'Sullivan to mark the Robert Emmet centenary, and himself proposed a motion similar to that passed in 1902 suspending any member playing or encouraging English games. However, as had happened in 1902, an amendment was passed (against Cusack's wishes) making this rule optional at the discretion of each county board. Cusack's last congress was that for 1905, held on 28 January 1906, ten months to the day before his death.

The first congress Cusack attended after the collapse of the *Celtic Times* was that of 1889, which witnessed Davin's second resignation as president and marked the second Fenian take-over of the GAA. Ostensibly Davin left because he felt he was being unfairly criticised for the financial failure of the 'American Invasion' tour of 1888. To his credit, Cusack was one of the minority who stoutly defended Davin. At the next convention Cusack attended, that for 1892, he supported a motion (which was heavily defeated) to hold future conventions in Dublin. At this same convention an application by him for a handicapper's licence was passed on to the next Dublin convention, but although the latter approved his application there is no record of its being granted by the central council.[20]

Between the congresses of 1889 and 1892, Cusack (again as a Dublin delegate) took part in a special delegate meeting of the GAA held in the Rotunda, Dublin, in July 1891. The ostensible purpose of this was to consider what steps were required to 're-organise and unify' the 'scattered forces' of the GAA, and the main decision taken was to set up a special committee to advise on the rules and on re-structuring the administration. Cusack was one of nine members of this committee, which produced a detailed report that led to some important changes both in rules and in administration being made by the next congress, held in January 1892. At the Rotunda, Cusack also supported a motion by P. N. Fitzgerald to appoint a paid secretary to the central council.

Cusack's sudden return to prominence in the GAA in 1891 was to be of short duration, and can easily be explained as exceptional. The widespread episcopal and clerical condemnations that had followed the second Fenian take-over of 1889 had caused the Association to go into so steep a decline that Cusack obviously felt it his duty to forget any personal or policy differences he had with the executive when the future of the GAA was at stake. In addition, his strong pro-Parnell stance from 1890 had brought him back into temporary prominence in Dublin GAA affairs, since the Dublin board had become a rallying point for Parnellite support in the capital. The July 1891 delegate meeting itself was, indeed, used by prominent Parnellites in the Association to secure the adoption of a blatantly partisan and political motion supporting Parnell's leadership of the Home Rule movement.

His prominence in 1891 notwithstanding, however, the fact remains that for the ten years from 1888 to 1898 Cusack was invariably at odds with the GAA leaders. This meant that, apart from the 1893 and 1901 episodes, he had to be content to express his dissatisafaction with Association policy through occasional (and sometimes characteristically vicious) letters to the newspapers. For most of this period his main criticism related to what he regarded as the GAA's too close, unjustifiable and unnecessary co-operation with the IAAA, amounting at times (according to him) to dictation to the GAA through the IAAA from what he regarded as its parent body, the AAA in England. However, successive central councils, right into the early years of the present century, continued to ignore Cusack on this major topic, and co-operation with the IAAA was regarded as unavoidable. It is easy to undertand that as the two field games sponsored by the GAA gradually came to dominate its calendar, the common-sense view prevailing on the central council was that peaceful co-existence with the IAAA had to be tolerated lest control of athletics be wrested from the GAA althogher. But then compromise was a concept totally alien to Cusack's temperament.[21]

Around 1898, a perceptible change occurred in Cusack's attitude to the GAA executive. The most noticable manifestation of this change was to be found in both the frequency and the tone of his intermittent letters to the papers. In a characteristic outburst in 1896, in which he accused the central council of that year as being 'un-Irish', he continued, 'I may be preaching in the wilderness, but I'll go on preaching all the same.' By 1898, he had, however, stopped doing so, and the small number of letters he sent to the press thereafter were either complimentary or constructive in their comments on the GAA and its progress. Typical of these is one of the last he had published, in January 1905, when he reviewed the GAA's successes in recent years, emphasised its role in the recent cultural revival and wound up in reminiscent mood on his associations with Michael Davitt when starting the GAA.[22]

This mellowing of Cusack's character and temperament coincided with the start of a shift of power within the GAA itself — the move towards reform that led, first to the setting up of provincial councils in 1900, and then in 1901 to the election as president and secretary of Nowlan and O'Toole. It is impossible to avoid the conclusion that there was some connection between Cusack's change of attitude and the rise of the younger men in the GAA. What seems to have happened was that Cusack found that, both in their general views on how the Association should be run and in their political outlook, the new men coming to the top were more to his liking than the majority of those who had been in charge of the GAA since his dismissal.

There is, however, no evidence that men like Nowlan and O'Toole and their associates took Cusack into their confidence. His occasional public statements from 1898 onwards reveal little more than that he knew of the reformers' plans and approved of them. It must be remembered, too, that, despite the changes in personnel on the central council from 1901 onwards, some of the older men continued to exert influence on GAA policy; and to some of them even a mellowed Cusack would not be welcome. It is noticeable that the committee that organised the testimonial on his behalf in 1902 consisted largely of old colleagues of his on the Dublin board, and that even of these only Tobin had been on the central council. The absence of Dineen, and the absence of any letters from Cusack in *Sport* when Dineen took over its GAA column after Sutton's death in 1900, are significant in this context.

One of the more pathetic aspects of Cusack's support for the new GAA was the manner in which he went out of his way to emphasise his credentials as an old Fenian of the 1860s, something that he must have known would endear him to men like T. F. O'Sullivan, then active in a rejuvenated IRB. Several times in the few letters or articles Cusack wrote around the turn of the century — in 1897, 1898 and 1901 — he re-stated his allegiance to the physical force movement of his early days. So successful was he in these protests of loyalty to the concept of physical force that some of those who knew Cusack only in his last few years became convinced that he had been sworn into the new IRB of the early years of this century. Among these were Bulmer Hobson of Belfast and Pat Devlin ('Celt') of Armagh. In fact, it is safe to assume that the screening process then invariably used would have kept Cusack out in any event.

To those mainly interested in Michael Cusask as the pioneer of the revival of Gaelic games, it has for long been a source of embarrassment that the most detailed surviving portrait of him is to be found in the character known as the Citizen in the writings of James Joyce and Oliver St John Gogarty. To Joyce the Cusack depicted in *Ulysses* was not merely a typical Fenian in outlook and temperament; he was also a bigoted, prejudiced, narrow-minded and even dissolute nationalist. Gogarty's portrait of Cusack, on the other hand, is noticeably more sympathetic and easier to recognise as the Cusack who emerges from his numerous letters to the newspapers in the 1890s.

However, *Ulysses* only began to be widely circulated in 1934, and Gogarty's *Tumbling in the Hay* first appeared in 1939. By then, of course, most of Cusack's intimates were dead. As a result, anyone wishing in the past half-century to test, much less to challenge, the accuracy of these two famous thinly-disguised portraits of Cusack has been obliged to concentrate largely on searching for inconsistencies or inaccuracies, based on what is known about the Cusack with whom both writers were acquainted.

The Cusack described by Joyce in Chapter XII of *Ulysses* bears little more than a faint resemblance to the only Cusack Joyce could have known — during his undergraduate period in UCD, from 1898 to 1902. Furthermore, there is reliable evidence that in the last four years of his life (1902 to 1906), when Joyce was still at least intermittently in touch with the Dublin he only finally left in 1904, the real Michael Cusack was in hardly any respect similar to the boisterous character who dominates the famous Cyclops episode of Chapter XII of *Ulysses*.

At the same time, it has been clear since 1975 that anyone arguing that the Citizen contains nothing of Cusack can be proved wrong by the best possible evidence. For in that year Myron Schwartzmann, now Professor of English at Baruch College in the City University of New York, published his seminal 78-page analysis of what is accepted as being the first draft of the Cyclops episode.[23] Since then champions of Cusack can no longer make any capital out of the omission of his name from the published text. For Schwartzmann demonstrates (with copious extracts, and even photographs, from Joyce's notebook) that 'Citizen Cusack' was the original or model on which the Citizen was based. Moreover, as recently as 1983 it transpired that it was less than a year after Cusack's death in December 1906 that Joyce first put together the

Neary & Neul
1 Great Strand St
Dublin
Jan. 14th 1900

My dear Citizen L. S. Mangan:

Kindly tell the boy whose name
is mentioned in this day's London
Correspondence of the Freeman
as the winner of the £50 prize
how glad I am of his success.

Believe me, my excellent friend
that I have taken a hearty interest
in everything Irish that you and
yours have taken a part in,
not only since I first heard you
in public in the Square in fort
now some thirty one years ago,
but even from the first
dawn of reason.

Yours Faithfull
Michael Cusack

A Cusack letter of 1900, to 'Citizen' Mangan

nucleus of the material for the Cyclops episode, although he did not get down to writing it until the summer and autumn of 1919.[24]

Schwartzmann's examination of Joyce's handwritten notes is not, however, without some consolation for admirers of Cusack. For it enables them to explain why Joyce omitted the surname from the published book. By the time *Ulysses* was ready for publication he had added so much to the character of the Citizen that he realised that it now bore little resemblance to the Cusack he had known some fifteen or twenty years before. So little of Cusack, even as seen through the undergraduate Joyce's cynical and irreverent eyes at the turn of the century, remained that it would have been pointless, perhaps misleading even for one so insensitive as Joyce, to retain the surname.

In trying to ascertain how close Joyce's Citizen comes to the real Cusack, it is surely essential to accept that what the writer was engaged in was not satire but caricature. Here, however, Cusack's admirers face the unpalatable fact that the essence of caricature (as we all know from modern newspaper cartoons) is the exaggeration of a personal characteristic that exists in the person caricatured. Indeed, anyone who has familiarised himself with Cusack's numerous letters to the papers is forced to admit that, even when allowance is made for the element of caricature, some of the things Joyce's Citizen said and did do ring true (if only faintly at times), and do remind one of Cusack. Moreover, one of the merits of Schwartzmann's essay, as well as of another American's examination, around the same time, of the changes Joyce made during 1919 to the Cyclops chapter, is that both reveal how close to the pre-1898 Cusack the original draft was before Joyce began almost to smother it in alterations.[25]

And yet ... When one's suspicions about the accuracy of Joyce's original portrait of Cusack are admitted, there still remains an unanswered question: How did Joyce come to depict a Cusack he could not have known? For 1898, it can be shown, did not merely mark the beginning of a Michael Cusack at last in tune with the GAA. That year, too, a certain change of temperament occurred in Cusack. Suddenly, after a quarter of a century, he gave up quarrelling with people, and a new Cusack emerged.

This new Cusack could present his walking-stick and his watch (the one he did not pawn when his paper collapsed?) to two friends after the humiliating chair-pulling incident in Thurles in 1902. This new Cusack could respond with almost paternal tenderness when accosted on the Dublin quays in 1906 by two Protestant boys who had found Rosary beads in the street. This new Cusack could publicly acknowledge the sympathetic reception he received at the 1905 congress after the death of a son. This new Cusack could publicly admit to being overwhelmed by the grant of £50 by the same congress in recognition of the unpaid work he had done as secretary of the GAA in its first eighteen months, before his dismissal twenty years before.[26]

Nor is that the end of the matter. To try to equate Joyce's Citizen — aggressive, morose, pugnacious, the worst for wear from alcohol by mid-afternoon — with the Cusack we know began again around 1900 to play an active role in the Dublin GAA is quite impossible. For those last seven years of his life, Cusack took a leading part in the new Dublin Hurling League, a semi-independent unit of the Dublin board with its own committee and officers, that was responsible for the spread of hurling throughout the city and county. He also, as we know, attended four congresses of the GAA as an elected Dublin delegate, and in 1904 travelled to Belfast on GAA business, an occasion vividly recalled sixty years later for this writer by Bulmer Hobson, who described Cusack as 'a vigorous vital old man'.[27]

What makes the mystery of Joyce's Citizen even more curious is the knowledge that Joyce did know another Cusack. For in one other work of semi-autobiography by Joyce we get glimpse of a very different Cusack from the Citizen of *Ulysses*. While the average reader is unlikely to make anything out of the two cryptic references to Cusack in Joyce's last book *Finnegans Wake,* there is one brief account of Cusack in Joyce's *Portrait of the Artist as a Young Man.* Stephen Dedalus's (or Joyce's) fellow-student at the university, Davin (in reality George Clancy of Limerick) had, we are told, met 'Michael Cusack, the Gael'. According to Joyce's biographer, Richard Ellmann, Clancy had brought Joyce to meet Cusack several times, perhaps (another reference in the *Portrait* would suggest) at the famous back-room in Cathal McGarvey's tobacco shop 'An Stad' in Dublin, where we know Griffith met his cronies, including (we know from Gogarty) Cusack.[28]

Joyce's *Portrait*, we now know, was a drastically-revised version of an earlier manuscript which, rescued from his papers, was published in 1944, thirty years after the *Portrait* itself, as *Stephen Hero.* In this latter book is to be found a much more recognisable depiction of Cusack, attending weekly Irish classes in the back-room of a house in central Dublin. He was stout, black-bearded, always wore a wide awake hat and a long bright green muffler. He had a loud voice and was always scoffing. When Joyce (Dedalus again) asked his friend Madden (Davin of the *Portrait*) what was the point of the hurling games in the Phoenix Park, Madden, clearly echoing Cusack, explained that the *camáns* would improve the physique of the country.

As for Gogarty's treatment of Cusack, if admirers of the GAA's founder find Joyce's Cyclops chapter embarrassing, they have good reason to be outraged by *Tumbling in the Hay*. However, a closer reading of Gogarty's rabelaisian novel forces one to the conclusion that in his Citizen, Gogarty has rolled two characters into one, only one of which is Cusack.

About one-fifth of the way through Gogarty's book comes what is clearly an authentic account of a session in McGarvey's 'An Stad'. Here in the company of Arthur Griffith and Sean T. O'Kelly (a future President of Ireland) is the real Michael Cusack, not only called by his own name but described in detail. In language noticeably less abrasive than Joyce's, Gogarty gives what one survivor of that period who visited 'An Stad' many times assured this writer forty years later is an accurate depiction of the place.[29]

Elsewhere, but attributed to the non-Cusack part of Gogarty's Citizen, one has little difficulty in picking out attributes Gogarty borrowed from Cusack. His ability to break the silence of a group with his ejaculatory news, the way he called all his friends 'Citizen', his crude comment on Nelson (reminding one of Cusack's view of Wellington in 1887) — all were almost certainly the result of Gogarty's observation of Cusack around the same time as Joyce had known him.[30]

'The rebel can reckon upon nothing in life ... but let him once go out of life, and he is sure of a fine funeral.' So wrote the Fenian leader (and GAA patron) John O'Leary in his memoirs in 1896.[31] One is reminded of this cynical but shrewd comment on reading the newspaper reports of the funeral of Michael Cusack, who died unexpectedly on 28 November 1906, some four months short of his sixtieth birthday.[32]

Sunday 2 December 1906 was a dull murky day in Dublin, an ideal excuse for not attending a funeral. Yet the GAA, to whose leaders one suspects their founder had become something of an embarrassment in recent years, turned out in force to swell the cortege to Glasnevin cemetery. By a stroke of luck, the hurlers of

Tipperary and Kilkenny were in town for a game and, wearing mourning rosettes and with *camáns* reversed, they marched alongside the hearse all the way from the Pro-Cathedral. Behind them came a hundred hurlers from Dublin, the county where he had begun the hurling revival and where he had always had his most loyal associates in the GAA.

A full turn-out of the GAA central council, headed by Alderman Jim Nowlan, led the procession. From Dublin Corporation came a handful of Sinn Féin members. The young were well represented too — by a uniformed party of Countess Markievicz's Fianna Eireann, and by an even younger group of juvenile players from central Dublin, who all carried either tiny *camáns* or footballs. Leading the graveside prayers was a young curate, Fr John Flanagan, kinsman of another Dublin 'character', the 'Bird Flanagan' — a priest whose political sympathies were to become public ten years later when he ministered inside the GPO during the Easter Rising. On the coffin, it was observed in the pale sunlight as it was lowered into the earth beside that of Cusack's wife, was the inscription 'Micheal Ciosóg — Tuismitheoir Chumann na nCleas Luith Gaedheal; 1847–1906'.

Footnotes

1. See, e.g. letter referred to in n. 3, Chapter 2.
2. See Cusack in *Chicago Citizen,* 24.9.1888.
3. The writer wishes to acknowledge the debts he owes, to Breandán O hEithir for putting him on the trail of the incomplete file of the *Celtic Times,* and to the anonymous owner of the file for permitting it to be examined and notes to be taken. This file contains in bound form Nos 8 to 22 and 48 to 53. Copies of Nos 41 to 47, found by the writer among Davin's papers (in the possession of the Walsh family of Carrick-on-Suir) are now in the National Library. Still missing are nine issues, viz Nos 1 to 8 & 54. This writer is satisfied from internal evidence that the set of twenty-one issues in anonymous ownership was originally owned by his grandfather, J. J. Bourke of Tipperary, whose family after his death in 1918 gave the set to the GAA historian, T. F. O'Sullivan. The set eventually came into the possession of the late Mr Tommy Moore of Cathedral Street, Dublin, chairman of Faughs H C, from whom their present owner acquired them.
4. See T. W. Moody: *Davitt and Irish Revolution, 1846–1882,* (Oxford, 1982), pp. 413, 414, 525-527.
5. See *Dictionary of American Biography,* 1909 edition, Vol. VII.
6. See *Sport,* 12.7.1919.
7. See Cusack in *Daily Nation,* 29.1.1898.
8. Con Short; *The Ulster GAA Story* (Rassan, 1984), pp. 37 & 39. See also *Glensmen,* Nos 2 & 9, Vol. 1 (June 1931 & 1932), and O Ceallaigh: *Gaelic Athletic Memories* (Dublin, 1945), p. 109.

9. See *Irish Daily Independent*, 16.12.1893 and *FJ*, 22.11.1984.
10. *Parnellite*, 16.3.1895.
11. See de Búrca: *Gaelic Games in Leinster* (1984), pp. 1-6.
12. *United Irishman*, 13.1.1900.
13. *FJ*, 13.6.1902.
14. *Gaelic Athletic Annual & County Directory*, 1907-1908, opp. p. 35.
15. R. Ellmann (ed.): *Letters of James Joyce* (London, 1966), Vol. II, pp. 209-210.
16. Mr Michael Foley, 2 Peckford Terrace, Dublin 1, to the writer, 1987.
17. See note 13.
18. *Gaelic Athlete*, 3.4.1915.
19. *FJ*, 13.6.1902; *Camán*, 1.6.1932.
20. See *FJ*, 10.3.1892.
21. See *Irish Daily Independent*, 2.2.1895 and *Nation*, 25.1.1890.
22. *FJ*, 7.1.1905.
23. *James Joyce Quarterly*, Vol. 12, Nos. 1 & 2 (1974-75), pp. 64-122.
24. Rodney Wilson Owen: *James Joyce and the Beginnings of Ulysses*, (Michigan, 1983), pp. 4 & 110.
25. *James Joyce Quarterly*, Vol. 12, Nos. 1 & 2: *"Cyclops" in Progress*, 1919, by Michael Groden, pp. 123-168.
26. See *Clare Champion*, 2.10.1906.
27. Letter of 31.10.1965; see also *Gaelic Football*, ed. Carbery (Dublin, 1941), article by P. D. Mehigan.
28. For *Finnegans Wake* see pp. 49 & 550; for 'An Stad', see 'Celt' in *An Ráitheachán*, March 1937.
29. The late Michael Grace, engineer, of Oldcastle, Co Meath, later a prominent member of Sinn Féin; see also *Gaelic Football* (ed. Carbery, Dublin 1941), article by 'Celt'.
30. For Cusack on Wellington, see *CT*, No. 13 (26.3.1887).
31. *Recollections of Fenians & Fenianism*, Vol. 1, p. 152.
32. For Cusack's funeral, see *FJ*, 3.12.1906; *Sport*, 8.12.1906; *Gaelic American*, 22.12.1906.

Principal Sources

Celtic Times, 1887-88
Irish Sportsman, 1887
Sport, 1892, 1893, 1901
Freeman's Journal, 1887
Evening Herald, 1893
Irish Weekly Independent, 1901
Gaelic Athlete, 1915
Upton MS History of GAA (custody of Director-General of GAA)
T. F. O'Sullivan, *Story of the GAA* (Dublin, 1916)
GAA Central Council Minutes, Vol. I (1899-1911)
de Burca, *The GAA: A History* (Dublin 1980 & 1981)
Mandle, W.T., *The Gaelic Athletic Association & Irish Nationalist Politics, 1884-1924* (Dublin & London, 1987)
Ellmann, Richard, *James Joyce* (Oxford, 1983)

CLARE CLUBS

SUBSCRIPTION LIST

£200
Clare County Board
  (Communications
  Committee)

£50 EACH
Broadford
Clarecastle
Clooney
Cooraclare
Corofin
Crusheen
Doonbeg
Eire Og
Feakle
Kildysart
Kilmaley
Kilmihil
Kilmurry Ibrickane
Kilrush
Michael Cusacks
Newmarket-on-Fergus
O'Callaghan's Mills
Ruan
Sixmilebridge
Scariff
St. Breckan's
St. Joseph's (Doora Barefield)
St. Joseph's (Miltown Malbay)
St. Senan's
Shannon Gaels
Tulla
Wolfe Tones na Sionna

£30 EACH
An Droichead
Ballyea
Ballyvaughan
Banner
Bodyke
Clonbony
Clondegad
Clonlara
Coolmeen (Football)
Coolmeen (Hurling)
Cratloe
Doolin
Ennistymon (Football)
Ennistymon (Hurling)
Inagh
Kilfenora
Kilkee Béalatha
Killanena
Killimer
Kilnamona
Liscannor
Lissycasey
Meelick
Moy
Naomh Eóin
O'Currys
Ogonnelloe
Parteen
Smith O'Briens
St. Bridget's
Tubber
Whitegate

INDEX

186

PHOTOGRAPHIC ACKNOWLEDGEMENTS

Cover and frontispiece photographs of Michael Cusack and that of
Margaret Cusack (28) were loaned by Ms Pat O'Connell; the
Cusack homestead (8), Lough Cutra School (21), 11 Emmet Street
(33), 4 Gardiner's Place (40), P. W. Nally and Maurice Davin (49),
John McKay and John Wyse Power (136), all courtesy of the GAA;
the 'Citizen' letter (179), courtesy of the Mangan family.